Human Body

Fun Activities, Experiments, Investigations, and Observations!

Grades 2–3

Credits

Authors: Sue Carothers and Elizabeth Henke

Production: Quack & Company, Inc.

Illustrations: Carol Tiernon

Cover Design: Matthew VanZomeren

Photo Credit: LifeArt image © 2001, Lippincott Williams & Wilkins. All rights reserved.

This book has been correlated to state, national, and Canadian provincial standards. Visit *www.carsondellosa.com* to search for and view its correlations to your standards.

ISBN 0-88724-953-1

Table of Contents

Table of Contents

Introduction

Human Body is a useful and creative way for teachers and parents to enhance a textbook unit about the human body or present a unit if a textbook is not available.

The book includes an overview of each major body system that introduces and explains the organs and vocabulary relating to that system. To access prior knowledge and summarize concepts, a KWL chart is included for each system. Diagrams of the systems and of individual organs are also included for students to color and/or label. Crossword puzzles, magic squares, and word searches within each unit are fun ways to familiarize students with vocabulary, improve spelling skills, and develop language arts skills while learning interesting facts. Many of these exercises can also be used for assessment purposes.

To reinforce and strengthen students' understanding of concepts, a variety of activities, investigations, observations, demonstrations, and models are included. These projects require few materials, include easy-to-follow directions, and are designed to be both educational and enjoyable.

Name _____

Building Blocks of the Body

Human bodies are made up of trillions of tiny building blocks called **cells**. Most cells are too small to be seen without using a microscope. There are over 200 different kinds of cells in the body. Each type of cell has a different shape and size, and each type has a different job to do in the body. At any moment, there are billions of cells in the body that die and are being replaced by new ones.

Cells in your body do not work alone. Cells of the same kind work together to make up tissue. A tissue is a group of cells that are alike and perform a certain job together. Just as the cells are grouped into tissues, the tissues of the body are grouped together into organs. Organs, such as your brain, heart, lungs, and stomach, are the main parts of the body and are arranged into systems. A system is a group of organs that work together to perform one or more jobs.

Color and label the types of cells that are shown by matching the numbers.

1. Color the **bone** cell yellow.   2. Color the **muscle** cell green.

3. Color the **epithelial** cell orange.   4. Color the **white blood** cell purple.

5. Color the **red blood** cell red.   6. Color the **nerve** cell blue.

1. _____
forms tissue that
makes bone

2. _____
forms tissue that
can stretch

3. _____
forms tissue that
covers and protects

4. _____
kills germs that
attack the body

5. _____
carries oxygen and
food to cells and
takes away carbon
dioxide

6. _____
carries messages to
and from the brain

Name _____

Systems of the Human Body
Mini-Book

Reproduce the mini-book on pages 5-8 for each student. Have the students cut the pages in half along the dashed line. Instruct the students to put the book in the following order: The Skeletal System, The Muscular System, The Digestive System, The Respiratory System, The Circulatory System, and The Nervous System. This order coincides with the order the systems are presented in this book. Staple the pages together along the left side to create books for the students to use as study guides. The first page of the mini-book can serve as a cover, but individual covers can also be made out of construction paper.

- -

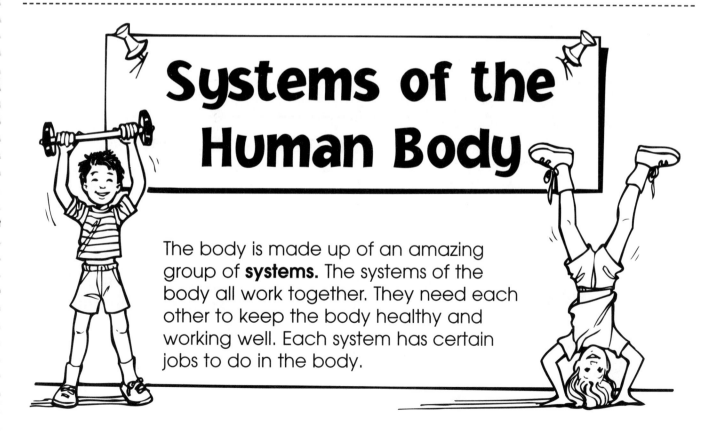

Systems of the Human Body

The body is made up of an amazing group of **systems.** The systems of the body all work together. They need each other to keep the body healthy and working well. Each system has certain jobs to do in the body.

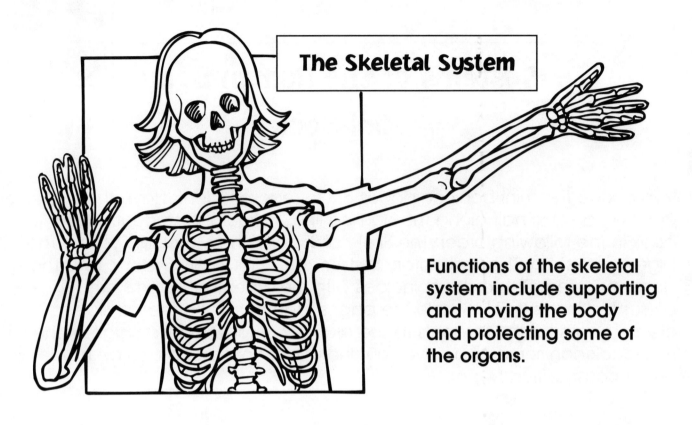

The Skeletal System

Functions of the skeletal system include supporting and moving the body and protecting some of the organs.

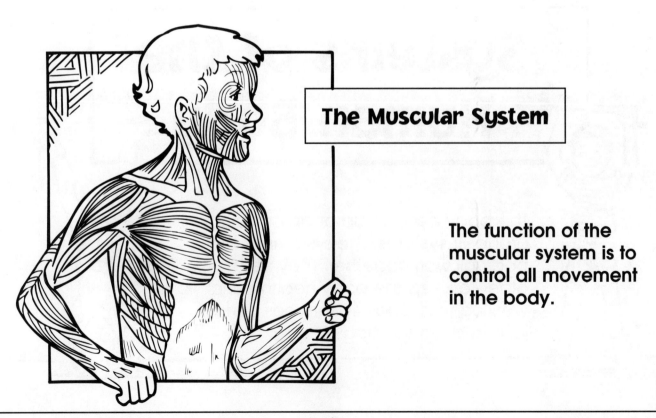

The Muscular System

The function of the muscular system is to control all movement in the body.

The Digestive System

One of the functions of the digestive system is to change food into a form that can be used by the body.

The Respiratory System

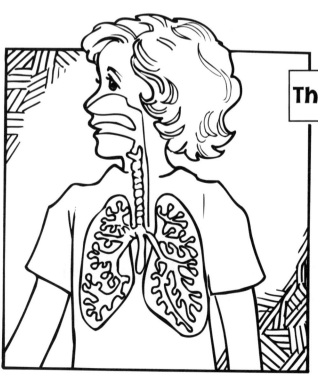

The function of the respiratory system is to bring in oxygen for the body to use and take away carbon dioxide.

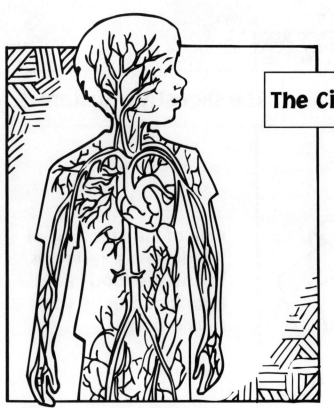

The Circulatory System

The main function of the circulatory system is to carry materials, such as food and oxygen, to the cells throughout the body.

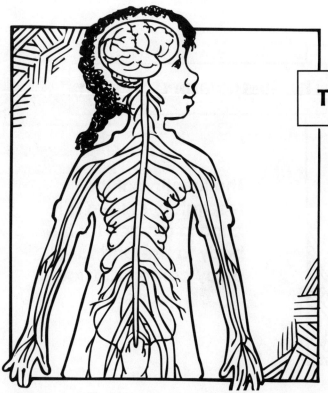

The Nervous System

An important function of the nervous system is to receive and carry messages to control the body.

8

Name _____

Organize Those Organs!

Each system of the body is made up of organs and body parts that work together. Each organ and body part does a certain job as part of the system.

Use the numbers to match each body part to a system of the body. Write the name of each part under the system to which it belongs.

Word Bank

stomach (3)	spinal cord (6)	small intestine (3)	nerves (6)
brain (6)	lungs (4)	trachea (4)	tendons (2)
muscles (2)	heart (5)	large intestine (3)	bones (1)
joints (1)	arteries (5)	diaphragm (4)	veins (5)

---

1. Skeletal System

_____

_____

_____

2. Muscular System

_____

_____

_____

3. Digestive System

_____

_____

_____

4. Respiratory System

_____

_____

_____

5. Circulatory System

_____

_____

_____

6. Nervous System

_____

_____

_____

Skeletal System

Muscular System

Digestive System

Respiratory System

Circulatory System

Nervous System

Name _____

Feeling Out of Place

There are many **organs** of the body. Each organ has a specific function or job to do. Organs work together to form **systems**.

For each system below, there are four body parts listed. Three of the body parts belong to that system; one does not. Circle the body part that does not belong in each system.

1. Respiratory System

   trachea   lungs   heart   diaphragm

2. Digestive System

   stomach   small intestine   mouth   ribs

3. Circulatory System

   heart   gallbladder   veins   arteries

4. Skeletal System

   large intestine   skull   ligaments   bones

5. Muscular System

   tendons   muscles   biceps   liver

6. Nervous System

   brain   spinal cord   pancreas   nerves

Name _____

The Body Matchers

A Memory Game

Instructions:

1. Cut out each of the cards below and the cards on pages 12-14. Some of the cards show the pictures and names of organs, and other cards show the name of a system of the body with a list of some of the major organs and body parts that belong to that system.

2. Once all the cards have been cut out, place the organ and body part cards in rows face down on the floor or a table. Place the system cards in a pile face down.

3. Decide who will go first. The first player turns over a system card. The player then turns over an organ and body parts card. If the card matches the system, the player keeps the card and turns over another card. If the card does not match the system, the card is turned back over, and it is the next player's turn.

4. When all the cards of a system are found, the player who found the final card turns over another system card.

5. Play continues until all cards have been matched. The player with the most cards is the winner.

Circulatory System	Respiratory System	Digestive System
heart	lungs	esophagus
veins	diaphragm	stomach
arteries	trachea	small intestine
capillaries	bronchial tubes	large intestine
		liver

Name _____

The Body Matchers

Muscular System

muscles

tendons

biceps

triceps

Nervous System

brain

spinal cord

nerves

Skeletal System

bones

skull

ribs

vertebrae

heart

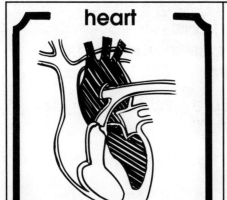

veins

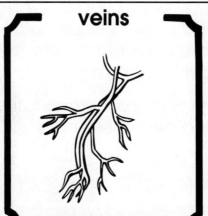

arteries

brain

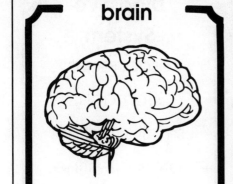

spinal cord

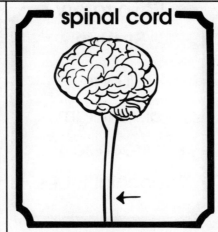

nerves

Name _____

The Body Matchers

capillaries

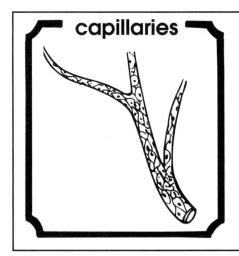

lungs

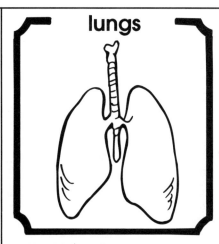

diaphragm

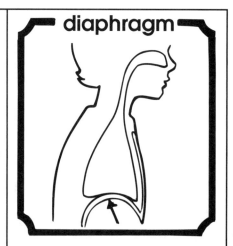

trachea

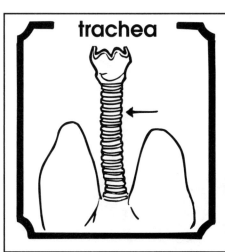

bronchial tubes

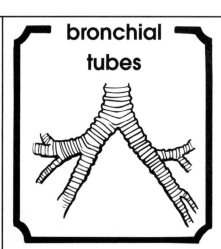

esophagus

stomach

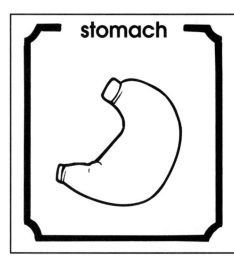

small intestine

large intestine

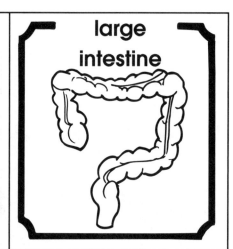

Name _____

The Body Matchers

liver	bones	skull
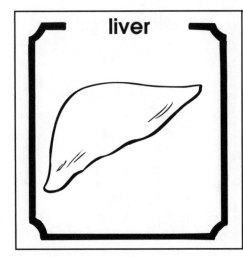	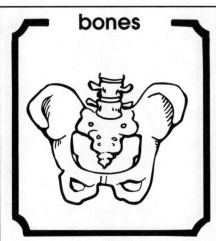	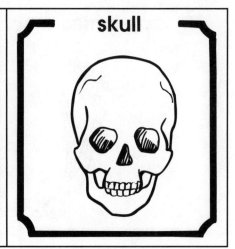

ribs	vertebrae	muscles
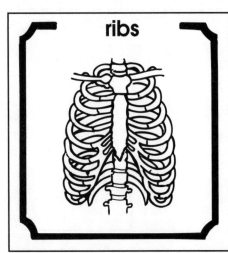	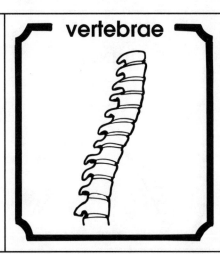	

tendons	biceps	triceps
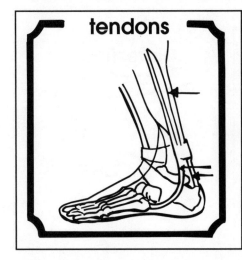	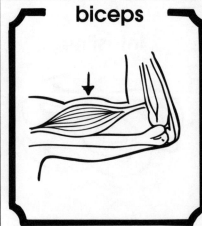	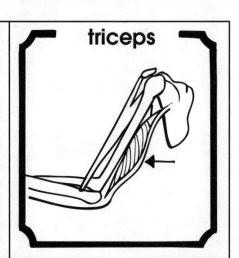

Name_____

KWL Chart
The Skeletal System

The skeletal system is the system that supports the body and gives it shape. It also protects the internal organs and, with the help of the muscles, allows the body to move. The main organs of the skeletal system are the bones.

Before you begin learning about the skeletal system, complete the first two sections of the chart below. Under **K**, list what you already know about the system. Under **W**, list what you would like to find out about the system. After you have studied the system, go back to the chart and list what you learned under **L**.

K What I know	W What I want to find out	L What I learned

Name _____

The Skeletal System

The skeletal system supports the body and gives it shape. Another function of the skeletal system is to work with muscles to move the body. A third function of the skeletal system is to protect the soft organs and body parts. For example, the **skull** protects the brain, while the **ribs** and **breastbone (sternum)** protect the lungs and heart. The backbone is made up of tiny bones called **vertebrae** that protect the spinal cord.

The skeleton is made up of 206 bones. Besides bones, the skeleton also has a type of rubbery tissue called **cartilage** in all the places where two bones meet. The cartilage cushions the bones and keeps them from rubbing together. The outer ear and the tip of the nose are very flexible because they are made up of cartilage.

The place where two or more bones join together, such as in the elbow or ankle, is called a **joint.** There are several different types of joints in the body. **Ligaments** connect the bones in the joints of the body and help to keep them in place.

Bones have a hard outer covering that is made up of tiny tubes. Nerves and blood vessels run through the tiny tubes of the outer layer. Underneath the outer layer is a hard, strong layer of bone cells that is surrounded by deposits of minerals such as calcium and phosphorous. The inner layer of bone is spongy with many air spaces.

In the very center of the bone is a large space filled with a type of tissue called **marrow.** Bone marrow is a soft tissue that makes new blood cells.

Answer each question.

1. What are the three functions of your skeletal system? _____

   _____

   _____

2. What is cartilage and where can it be found in your body? _____

   _____

3. What is the purpose of ligaments? _____

4. What is bone marrow? _____

Name _____

Name That Bone

Use the words from the Word Bank to label the diagram of the skeletal system.

Word Bank

skull

jawbone

ribs

upper arm bone

kneecap

neck bones

breastbone

calf bone

lower arm bone

backbone

hand bones

shinbone

foot bones

thighbone

hipbone

collarbone

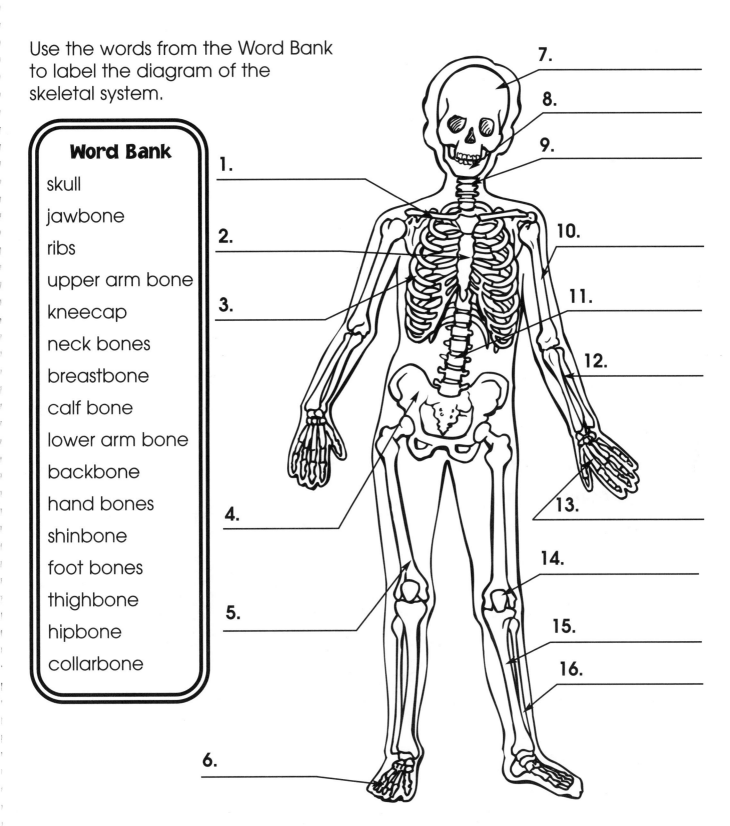

1.

2.

3.

4.

5.

6.

7.

8.

9.

10.

11.

12.

13.

14.

15.

16.

Name _____

No Bones About It

The outer part of the bones is made of a hard material called **compact bone**. Compact bone contains canals or tubes through which blood vessels and nerves run. The inner part of the bones consists of a layer of **spongy bone** which is filled with air spaces to make the bones lighter. Spongy bone contains **bone marrow** which makes **red blood cells** and stores fat for the body.

Draw a line to match the beginning of each sentence with its correct ending. Then follow the directions to color the picture below.

1. Compact bone

2. Blood vessels

3. Spongy bone

4. Bone marrow

a. makes red blood cells and stores fat.

b. is filled with bone marrow and air spaces.

c. is the hardest part of the bone.

d. bring new materials to bones to keep them strong and healthy.

Color the **compact bone** brown.

Color the **spongy bone** yellow.

Color the **bone marrow** pink.

Color the **blood vessels** red.

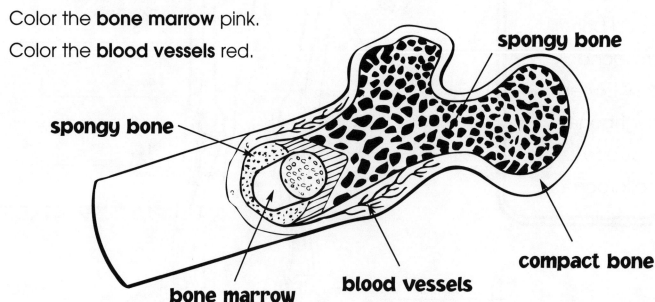

spongy bone

spongy bone

bone marrow

blood vessels

compact bone

Name _____

Joining Together

A **joint** is where two or more bones are joined together. There are many different kinds of joints in the body.

1. **Fixed joints**, as found in the skull, do not move. Label the fixed joint and color it blue.

2. **Ball-and-socket joints**, as found in the shoulder, allow the bones to swing in almost any direction. Label the ball-and-socket joint and color it green.

3. **Hinge joints**, like the joints in the elbow and knee, allow movement in one direction. Label the hinge joint and color it red.

4. **Pivot joints**, as found in the neck, form when one bone rests and rotates from a certain point. Label the pivot joint and color it orange.

5. **Gliding joints**, like in the wrist, are formed when two bones that can move separately meet. Label the gliding joint and color it yellow.

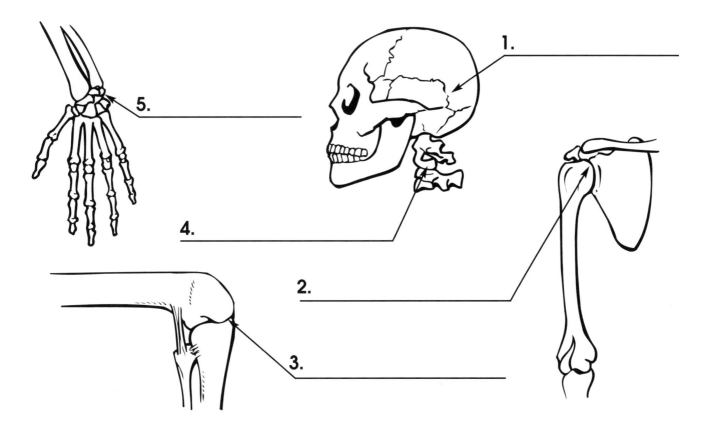

Name _____

Bone Up on the Skeletal System

Write **T** for true or **F** for false before each statement about the skeletal system. For each statement that is false, rewrite it on another piece of paper to make it a true statement.

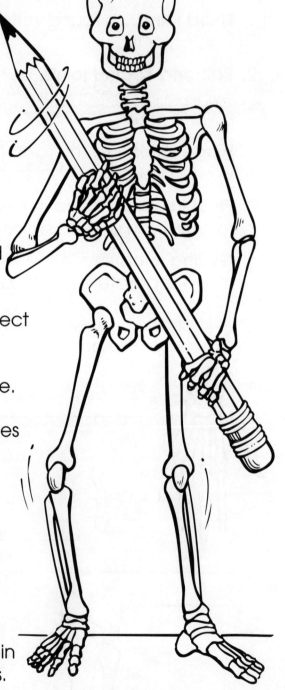

___ 1. The skeletal system supports the body and gives it shape.

___ 2. The skeletal system does not help the body move.

___ 3. The brain is protected by the skull.

___ 4. The lungs and heart are protected by the rib cage.

___ 5. Vertebrae are tiny bones that protect the spinal cord.

___ 6. Cartilage is another name for bone.

___ 7. The place where two or more bones join together is called a joint.

___ 8. A strong band of tissue that connects bones in the joints is called a ligament.

___ 9. Ligaments are made of calcium and phosphorous.

___10. Bone marrow is a soft tissue found in bones that makes new blood cells.

Name _____

I Did Not Know That!

Use the code to learn more about bones.

			Code			
A = 1	B = 2	C = 3	D = 4	E = 5	F = 6	G = 7
H = 8	I = 9	J = 10	K = 11	L = 12	M = 13	N = 14
O = 15	P = 16	Q = 17	R = 18	S = 19	T = 20	U = 21
V = 22	W = 23	X = 24	Y = 25	Z = 26		

1. At birth, there are about 350 of these. As the body grows, they fuse together. Adults only have 206 of these.

$$\overline{}\ \overline{}\ \overline{}\ \overline{}\ \overline{}$$
   2   15   14   5   19

2. Bone is five times stronger than a bar of the same weight made out of this.

$$\overline{}\ \overline{}\ \overline{}\ \overline{}\ \overline{}$$
   19   20   5   5   12

Now, that's interesting!

3. The largest bone, called the femur, is located in this part of the body.

$$\overline{}\ \overline{}\ \overline{}\ \overline{}\ \overline{}$$
   20   8   9   7   8

4. Nearly half of the bones are found in these parts of the body.

$$\overline{}\ \overline{}\ \overline{}\ \overline{}\ \overline{}$$ and $$\overline{}\ \overline{}\ \overline{}\ \overline{}$$
   8   1   14   4   19   6   5   5   20

5. The smallest bones are located in this part of the body. They are called the hammer, the anvil, and the stirrup.

$$\overline{}\ \overline{}\ \overline{}$$
   5   1   18

6. Even though this is called a bone, it is really a nerve that is found on the back of the elbow that is close to the bone. It is very painful when it gets hit.

$$\overline{}\ \overline{}\ \overline{}\ \overline{}\ \overline{}\qquad \overline{}\ \overline{}\ \overline{}\ \overline{}$$
   6   21   14   14   25   2   15   14   5

Name _____

A Skeletal Framework

Use the words from the Word Bank to complete the crossword puzzle.

Across

2. soft tissue inside the bones that makes new blood cells

4. connect the bones together and help keep joints in place

6. rubbery tissue in outer ear and nose tip

8. what makes up the skeleton

9. a "cap" of bones that protects the brain

Word Bank

skeleton joint bones

marrow ligaments

cartilage ribs skull

vertebrae

Down

1. the place where two or more bones come together

3. tiny bones that make up the backbone and protect the spinal cord

5. made up of all the bones in the body

7. bones that protect the lungs

Name _____

Digging for Bones

Circle the words from the Word Bank in the puzzle. The words appear horizontally and vertically.

Word Bank

anklebones	feet bones	leg bones	skeletal system
arm bones	hand bones	ligaments	skull
breastbone	hipbones	marrow	vertebrae
cartilage	joint	ribs	wrist bones
collarbone	kneecap	shoulder blades	

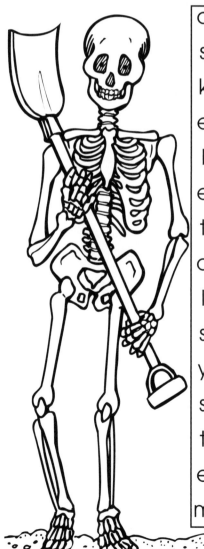

a	j	o	i	n	t	r	w	d	a	e	r	l	w
s	h	o	u	l	d	e	r	b	l	a	d	e	s
k	a	c	o	l	l	a	r	b	o	n	e	s	r
e	n	a	w	i	e	g	a	m	a	r	r	o	w
l	d	r	e	g	r	j	r	e	e	j	h	r	v
e	b	t	r	a	t	o	m	r	n	o	i	t	e
t	o	i	e	m	h	i	b	g	t	i	p	f	r
a	n	l	l	e	g	b	o	n	e	s	b	e	t
l	e	a	f	n	e	r	n	e	d	e	o	e	e
s	s	g	h	t	d	o	e	r	c	n	n	t	b
y	k	e	e	s	k	d	s	n	e	t	e	b	r
s	u	w	r	i	s	t	b	o	n	e	s	o	a
t	l	r	i	b	r	e	a	s	t	b	o	n	e
e	l	i	b	a	n	k	l	e	b	o	n	e	s
m	e	s	s	k	n	e	e	c	a	p	e	s	p

Name_____

KWL Chart
The Muscular System

The muscular system is the system that controls all movement in the body. Some of the main types of muscle are skeletal muscle, smooth muscle, and cardiac muscle.

Before you begin learning about the muscular system, complete the first two sections of the chart below. Under **K**, list what you already know about the system. Under **W**, list what you would like to find out about the system. After you have studied the system, go back to the chart and list what you learned under **L**.

K What I know	W What I want to find out	L What I learned

Name _____

The Muscular System

The muscular system is made up of all the different muscles that cause movement. There are more than 600 different muscles in the body that all control movement in some way. The two main types of muscles in the body are **involuntary muscles** and **voluntary muscles**. Involuntary muscles are muscles that cannot be consciously controlled. These are muscles, such as in the heart and stomach, that work without you needing to think about it. Voluntary muscles are muscles, such as the muscles in the arms, legs, and face, that are under conscious control. This means that the movement of voluntary muscles can be controlled. Voluntary muscles are also called skeletal muscles because they are attached to the bones of the skeleton. Skeletal muscles move your bones by working in opposing pairs. When a muscle contracts, it pulls the bone in one direction. When the opposite muscle contracts, it pulls the bone back in the other direction. Skeletal muscles are attached to the bones by tough bands called **tendons**.

Each muscle in the body is made up of a special kind of muscle tissue. There are three different kinds of muscle tissue: **skeletal muscle, smooth muscle**, and **cardiac muscle**. **Skeletal muscle** is striped and makes up the skeletal muscles of the body. Skeletal muscle is voluntary since its movement can be controlled. **Smooth muscle** is not striped, and it makes up the walls of many of the organs in the body such as the stomach and intestines. Smooth muscle is involuntary since its movement cannot be controlled. **Cardiac muscle** is the muscle tissue that is found in the heart. It is striped like the skeletal muscle, but it is involuntary.

Answer each question.

1. What is the purpose of the muscular system? _____

   _____

2. What is the difference between a voluntary muscle and an involuntary muscle? _____

3. How do the muscles cause the bones to move? _____

   _____

4. What are the three types of muscle tissue in the body? _____

   _____

Name _____

Show Your Muscles

Use the words from the Word Bank to label the muscle groups in the diagram of the muscular system.

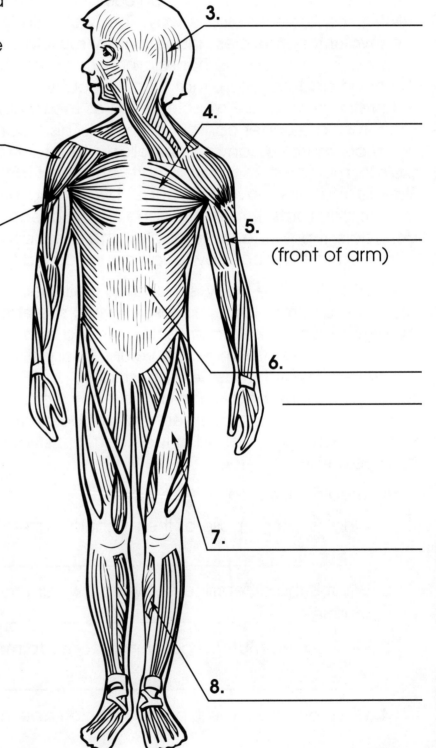

3. _____

4. _____

1. _____

5. _____

(front of arm)

2. _____

(back of arm)

6. _____

_____

7. _____

8. _____

Word Bank

chest muscles

shoulder muscles

stomach muscles

calf muscles

biceps

head muscles

thigh muscles

triceps

Name _____

Muscle Tissue

Draw a line to match the beginning of each sentence with its correct ending. Then write the name of each different type of muscle tissue in the box above the picture it names.

1. Skeletal muscle

2. Smooth muscle

3. Cardiac muscle

a. is not striped. It makes up the walls of the stomach, intestines, and other hollow organs of the body.

b. is striped muscle tissue that is found in the heart.

c. is striped muscle that is attached to the bones.

4.

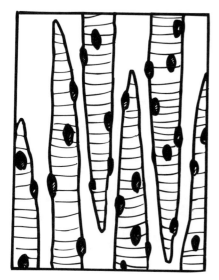

5.

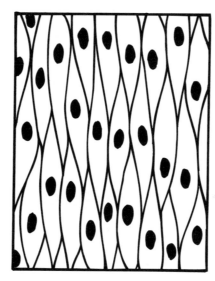

6.

Name _____

Muscle Up

Write **T** for true or **F** for false before each statement about the muscular system. For each statement that is false, rewrite it on another piece of paper to make it a true statement.

___ 1. There are over 600 muscles in the body that help with movement.

___ 2. Voluntary muscle and involuntary muscle are the two main types of muscle.

___ 3. Voluntary muscles, like those in the arm or leg, cannot be controlled.

___ 4. Involuntary muscles, like the heart, work automatically.

___ 5. Tendons are bones.

___ 6. Skeletal muscle is attached to bones.

___ 7. Smooth muscle is found in hollow organs of the body, such as the stomach.

___ 8. Cardiac muscle is found in your heart.

Name _____

What About My Muscles?

Use the code to learn some interesting facts about muscles.

Code

A = 1	B = 2	C = 3	D = 4	E = 5	F = 6	G = 7
H = 8	I = 9	J = 10	K = 11	L = 12	M = 13	N = 14
O = 15	P = 16	Q = 17	R = 18	S = 19	T = 20	U = 21
V = 22	W = 23	X = 24	Y = 25	Z = 26		

1. The 40 muscles in this part of the body allow people to express their feelings without using any words.

   ___ ___ ___ ___
    6   1   3   5

2. This tendon attaches the calf muscle in the leg to the heel bone and carries the whole weight of the body.

   ___ ___ ___ ___ ___ ___ ___ ___   ___ ___ ___ ___ ___ ___
    1   3   8   9 12 12   5 19   20   5 14   4 15 14

3. There are about 600 of these attached to bones. They can only pull the bones. They cannot push them.

   ___ ___ ___ ___ ___ ___ ___
   13 21 19   3 12   5 19

4. Muscles need this gas in order to do work. The harder muscles work, the more of this gas they need.

   ___ ___ ___ ___ ___ ___
   15 24 25   7   5 14

5. The body automatically does this when it is cold. It is caused by the involuntary contractions of muscles to give off heat to warm up the body. It can cause teeth to chatter.

   ___ ___ ___ ___ ___ ___ ___
   19   8   9 22   5 18 19

6. This is the name of the upper arm muscles that bodybuilders like to show off.

   ___ ___ ___ ___ ___ ___
    2   9   3   5 16 19

Name _____

Muscle Mania

Circle the words from the Word Bank in the puzzle. The words appear horizontally and vertically.

Word Bank

cardiac	skeletal	tendons
triceps	involuntary	smooth
voluntary	muscle	biceps

```
i  s  k  e  l  e  t  a  l  c
n  m  n  d  e  r  e  q  a  i
v  o  l  u  n  t  a  r  y  t
o  o  m  h  r  h  b  e  t  e
l  t  u  b  i  c  e  p  s  n
u  h  s  e  p  e  r  t  r  d
n  e  c  m  u  s  c  l  e  o
t  r  i  c  e  p  s  e  g  n
a  c  e  r  l  r  i  c  h  s
r  e  c  a  r  d  i  a  c  t
y  p  t  d  e  c  e  e  p  e
```

Name _____

Muscle Power

Use the words in the Word Bank to unscramble the words related to the muscular system.

Word Bank

cardiac	skeletal	tendons	move
involuntary	smooth	voluntary	muscle

1. what muscles help the body to do

   vmeo __ __ __ __

2. tissue that causes movement in the body

   cesuml __ __ __ __ __ __

3. the type of striped muscle that the heart is made of

   ardicca __ __ __ __ __ __ __

4. the type of muscle that can be controlled

   tyvunarlo __ __ __ __ __ __ __ __ __

5. the type of muscle that is striped and is attached to the bones for movement

   elelatsk __ __ __ __ __ __ __ __

6. the type of muscle that is not striped and makes up the walls of many of the organs in the body

   msthoo __ __ __ __ __ __

7. thick bands of tissue that attach muscles to bones

   ndontse __ __ __ __ __ __ __

8. muscles that move without being controlled

   nuitrvaloyn __ __ __ __ __ __ __ __ __ __ __

Name _____

Working in Pairs

Muscles move bones by pulling on them. When one muscle contracts, or gets shorter and fatter, it pulls the bone in one direction. The other muscle in the pair relaxes, or stretches out, when this happens. To move the bone the opposite way, the opposite muscle contracts while the other muscle of the pair relaxes. The muscles in the upper arm that work in a pair are called the bicep and the tricep.

Question:
How do your muscles work in pairs to move your arm?

Materials Needed:
- book
- table or desk

Procedure:

A. Rest your lower arm on a table or desk while you hold a book.

B. Put your opposite hand on the inside of your upper arm so you can feel your bicep.

C. Slowly lift the book off the table. Then, slowly lower the book back to the table. Notice what happens to your bicep.

D. Now place your hand on the back of your upper arm so you can feel your tricep.

Results:

Write down what you observed.

	lifting book	lowering book
bicep		
tricep		

Conclusions:

1. Which muscle contracts as you raise your forearm? _____

2. Which muscle contracts as you lower your forearm? _____

3. Describe how muscles work in pairs to move your bones. _____

_____

Name _____

KWL Chart
The Digestive System

The digestive system is the system that changes food into a form that can be used by the body. Some of the organs and body parts of the digestive system are the teeth, tongue, esophagus, stomach, small intestine, liver, gallbladder, pancreas, and large intestine.

Before you begin learning about the digestive system, complete the first two sections of the chart below. Under **K**, list what you already know about the system. Under **W**, list what you would like to find out about the system. After you have studied the system, go back to the chart and list what you learned under **L**.

K What I know	W What I want to find out	L What I learned

Name _____

The Digestive System

The purpose of the digestive system is to change food into a form that can be used by the cells of the body. The first steps of digestion take place in the **mouth** where the **teeth** break the food into smaller pieces and **saliva** is added to the food to make it wet and soft. As food is chewed, the **tongue** moves around in the mouth and mixes the food with saliva. Saliva is one of the many juices that mixes with the food along the path of digestion. The tongue also pushes the food to the back of the mouth when swallowing.

After swallowing, the food goes into a tube called the **esophagus**, which is lined with strong muscles to push the food to the **stomach**. The stomach is a J-shaped sac mostly made of muscles. In the stomach, the food is mixed with juices and squeezed and churned until it becomes a thick liquid.

Now the thick liquid food moves into the **small intestine**, which is a hollow tube about four times longer than your height. In the small intestine, food is mixed with more juices, some of which are made in the small intestine. The **liver** makes another juice and stores it in the **gallbladder** until it passes into the small intestine. The **pancreas** also makes and passes juices to the small intestine. On the inside of the small intestine are tiny, finger-shaped projections, called **villi**, that are lined with blood vessels. All of the food that can be used by the body goes into the blood from the small intestine. The blood carries this digested food to all the cells of the body.

The unused food and water that do not go into the blood from the small intestine pass to a wider, but shorter tube called the **large intestine**. Here, water is taken out of the food and is reabsorbed into the bloodstream. The remaining waste material leaves the body through an opening at the end of the large intestine.

Answer each question.

1. What is the purpose of the digestive system? _____

_____

2. What are the steps of digestion that occur in the mouth? _____

_____

3. What are the main organs of the digestive system? _____

_____

Name _____

Open Wide

Digestion begins in the mouth. Teeth help carry out the first step of digestion. The **incisors** are the teeth in front of the mouth. Incisors are thin, flat teeth with sharp edges to help cut and bite food. **Canines** are the pointed teeth located next to the incisors. Canine teeth have sharp points to bite and tear food. Next to the canines are the **premolars**. These teeth have flat tops which help to crush food into smaller pieces. In the back of the mouth are the **molars**. Molars have large, flat tops which help crush and grind food into smaller pieces.

Use words from the Word Bank to label the diagram of the upper and lower teeth. Color the incisors blue. Color the canines red. Color the premolars green, and color the molars yellow.

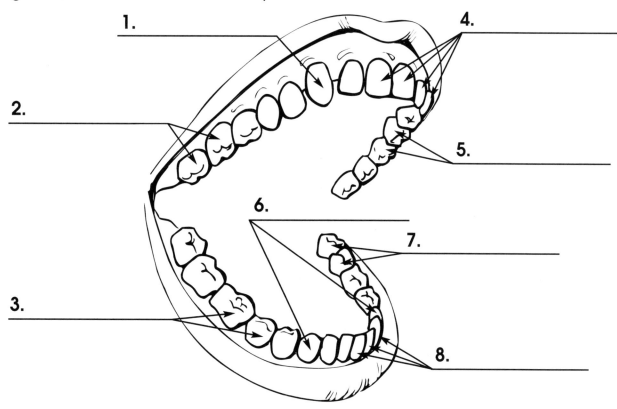

Word Bank

upper incisors	upper canine	upper premolars	upper molars
lower incisors	lower canines	lower premolars	lower molars

35

Name _____

Tooth Talk

The **crown** of the tooth is the part above the gum line. The **root** of the tooth is located under the gum. The outer covering of each tooth is called **enamel,** which is the hardest substance in the body. **Dentin** is a softer substance located underneath the enamel. Dentin helps to absorb the pressure or impact of chewing. Inside the dentin there is a **pulp chamber** containing **nerves** and **blood vessels** which nourish the tooth.

Bacteria feed on food particles in the mouth. When bacteria eat sugar, they produce an acid that dissolves the enamel, causing a cavity in the tooth.

Use the words from the Word Bank to label the parts of the tooth.

Word Bank

crown	enamel	nerves and blood vessels
dentin	root	pulp chamber

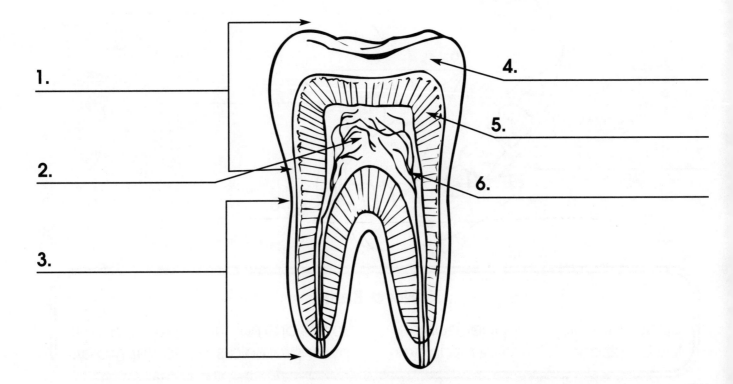

1. _____

2. _____

3. _____

4. _____

5. _____

6. _____

Name _____

The Hardest Substance

Use the words from the Word Bank to complete the following sentences. Then unscramble the letters in the circles to discover the name of the hardest substance in the body.

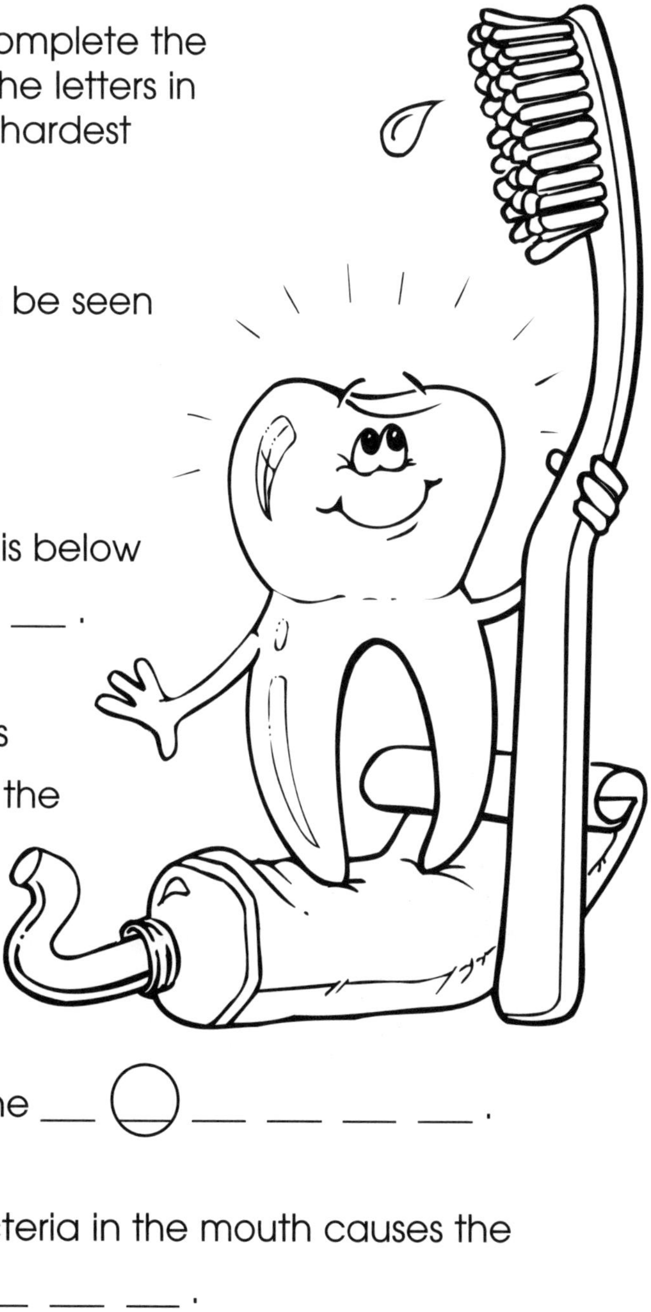

1. The top part of the tooth that can be seen above the gum is called the __ __ __ __ ◯ .

2. The bottom part of the tooth that is below the gum is called the __ __ __ __ .

3. The part of the tooth that contains nerves and blood vessels is called the __ __ ◯ __ __ __ ◯ __ ◯ __ .

4. The part of the tooth that absorbs the impact of chewing is called the __ ◯ __ __ __ __ .

5. The acid-producing action of bacteria in the mouth causes the tooth to develop a __ ◯ __ __ __ __ .

The hardest substance in the body is called __ __ __ __ __ __ .

Word Bank

cavity	crown	dentin	pulp chamber	root

Name _____

Functions of the Digestive System

Write the letter of each function of the digestive system next to the organ it describes.

Function

a. I store solid wastes and remove water from food. **What am I?**

b. I am the entrance where food enters the body. I chew up the food. **What am I?**

c. I am a muscular tube that squeezes food down to the stomach. **What am I?**

d. I am a J-shaped sac that stores food for a few hours while digestion occurs. **What am I?**

e. I am a hollow tube about four times longer than your height. Final digestion takes place here. **What am I?**

f. I am the largest organ inside the body. I make bile. **What am I?**

g. I hold the bile made by the liver. **What am I?**

h. I make pancreatic juice to help digest food. **What am I?**

Organs

1. mouth _____   2. esophagus _____   3. stomach _____

4. liver _____   5. pancreas _____   6. gallbladder_____

7. small intestine _____   8. large intestine _____

Name _____

A Colorful Food Path

Use the number code to label and color the diagram of the digestive system.

• • • • • • • • • • • • • • • • • **Number Code** • • • • • • • • • • • • • • • •

1. Color the **esophagus** blue.

2. Color the **liver** orange.

3. Color the **gallbladder** brown.

4. Color the **large intestine** black.

5. Color the **teeth** yellow.

6. Color the **tongue** pink.

7. Color the **stomach** green.

8. Color the **pancreas** purple.

9. Color the **small intestine** red.

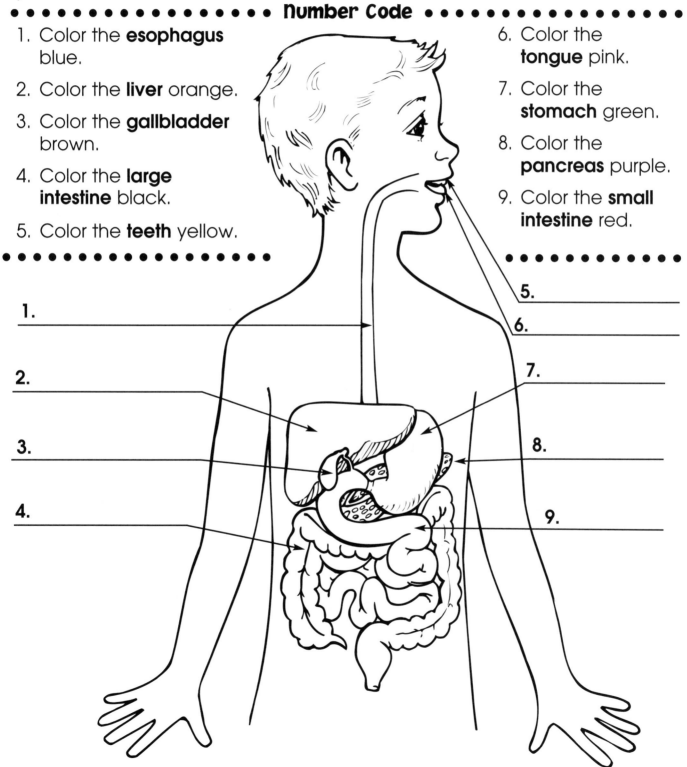

Name _____

Digestive Discoveries

Write **T** for true or **F** for false before each statement about digestion. For each statement that is false, rewrite it on another piece of paper to make it a true statement.

___ 1. Digestion begins in the esophagus.

___ 2. The esophagus connects the mouth to the stomach.

___ 3. The teeth and tongue are not part of the digestive system.

___ 4. There are no muscles in the stomach.

___ 5. The small intestine is about four times a person's height.

___ 6. Most of the digestion takes place in the small intestine.

___ 7. The liver and pancreas make juices that help digestion to occur.

___ 8. The large intestine is the longest part of the digestive system.

Name _____

Path of Digestion

Match each word or words in List I with its description from List II. Write the number in the box of the matching letter. To discover the magic number, add a row, column, or diagonal. The answer should always be the same!

List I

___ A. mouth

___ B. tongue

___ C. teeth

___ D. saliva

___ E. villi

___ F. esophagus

___ G. stomach

___ H. small intestine

___ I. large intestine

A.	B.	C.
D.	E.	F.
G.	H.	I.

Magic Number _____

List II

1. a fluid that keeps the mouth moist and makes food soft and wet when chewing

2. used for biting and chewing

3. a hollow tube that is about four times longer than a person's height

4. last section of the digestive tract; a hollow tube where water is removed from food

5. finger-like structures that line the small intestine

6. place where digestion begins

7. pushes food to the back of the mouth to be swallowed

8. j-shaped muscular sac that stores food and helps to digest it

9. a muscular tube that connects the back of the mouth to the stomach

Name _____

Fun Facts About the Digestive System

Use the code to learn some fun facts about the digestive system.

Code						
A = 1	B = 2	C = 3	D = 4	E = 5	F = 6	G = 7
H = 8	I = 9	J = 10	K = 11	L = 12	M = 13	N = 14
O = 15	P = 16	Q = 17	R = 18	S = 19	T = 20	U = 21
V = 22	W = 23	X = 24	Y = 25	Z = 26		

1. During a normal lifetime, the amount of food that a person eats is equal to the combined weight of six of these.

   ___ ___ ___ ___ ___ ___ ___ ___ ___
   5   12 5   16 8   1   14 20 19

2. These are caused when the stomach is empty and the stomach muscles squeeze together.

   ___ ___ ___ ___ ___ ___ ___   ___ ___ ___ ___ ___ ___
   19 20 15 13 1   3   8   7   18 15 23 12 19

3. An adult has 32 of these.

   ___ ___ ___ ___ ___
   20 5   5   20 8

4. Most of the length of the digestive system (80%) is made up of this organ. When stretched out, it is about four times longer than the body is tall.

   ___ ___ ___ ___ ___   ___ ___ ___ ___ ___ ___ ___ ___ ___
   19 13 1   12 12   9   14 20 5   19 20 9   14 5

5. About two pints (one liter) of this liquid is released into an adult's mouth each day.

   ___ ___ ___ ___ ___ ___
   19 1   12 9   22 1

6. This organ can stretch to hold about four pints (two liters) of food. The food spends about six hours here.

   ___ ___ ___ ___ ___ ___ ___
   19 20 15 13 1   3   8

Name _____

Just Passing Through

Circle the words from the Word Bank in the puzzle. The words appear horizontally and vertically.

Word Bank

digestion	juices	pancreas	teeth
esophagus	large intestine	saliva	tongue
food	liver	small intestine	villi
gallbladder	mouth	stomach	

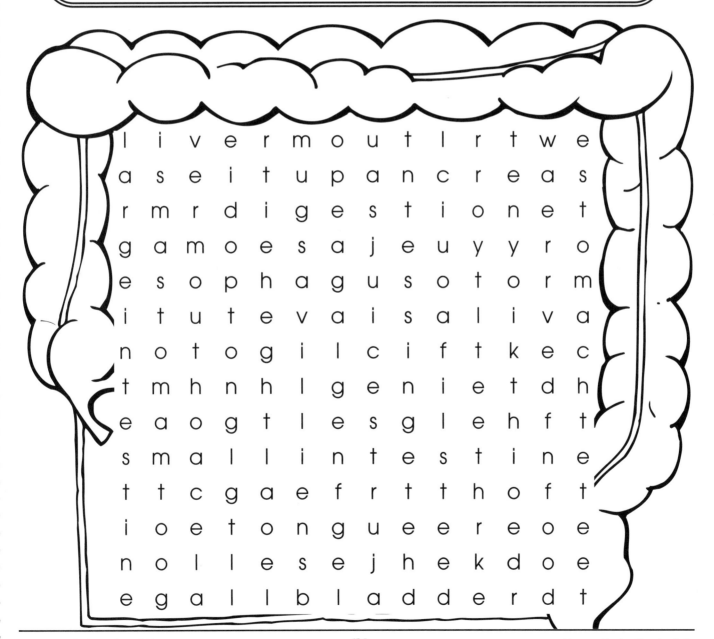

```
l i v e r m o u t l r t w e
a s e i t u p a n c r e a s
r m r d i g e s t i o n e t
g a m o e s a j e u y y r o
e s o p h a g u s o t o r m
i t u t e v a i s a l i v a
n o t o g i l c i f t k e c
t m h n h l g e n i e t d h
e a o g t l e s g l e h f t
s m a l l i n t e s t i n e
t t c g a e f r t t h o f t
i o e t o n g u e e r e o e
n o l l e s e j h e k d o e
e g a l l b l a d d e r d t
```

Name _____

The Digestive Organs

Use the words from the Word Bank to complete the puzzle. Match the numbered organs to the numbers in the puzzle.

Word Bank

| liver | mouth | esophagus | stomach |
| pancreas | gallbladder | large intestine | small intestine |

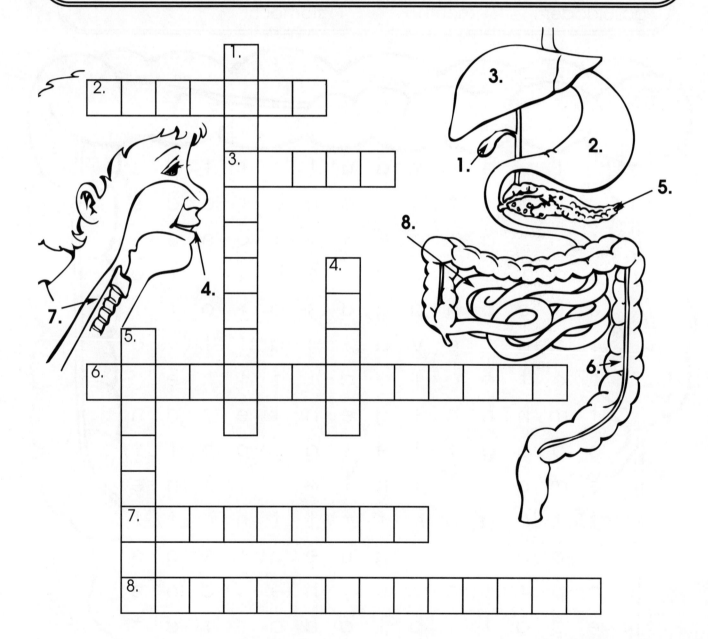

Name _____

The Path of Digestion

Below are sentences describing how the digestive system works. The sentences are not in the correct order. Number the sentences in the correct order.

_____ Food, in the form of a thick liquid, leaves the stomach and moves into the small intestine.

_____ First, food is taken in by your mouth where the teeth break the food into smaller pieces.

_____ Finally, your large intestine removes water from the food and adds it to the bloodstream. Waste material leaves the body through an opening at the end of the large intestine.

_____ The tongue mixes the food with saliva. The tongue also pushes the food to the back of the mouth to be swallowed.

_____ As teeth are breaking down the food, saliva is added to make the food soft and wet.

_____ When swallowing, food is pushed down by the muscles in the esophagus.

_____ In your small intestine food is mixed with more juices. Food is broken down into even smaller pieces. All the food that can be used by your body goes into the bloodstream.

_____ From the esophagus, food goes into the stomach where it is mixed with digestive juices.

_____ Unused food and water that do not go into the bloodstream from the small intestine go into the large intestine.

_____ Stomach muscles squeeze and churn the food and juices to form a thick liquid.

Name _____

Starchy or not?

Carbohydrates are foods that the body needs for energy. **Starch** is one kind of carbohydrate that is found in many foods. You can test to see if starch is present in foods by using iodine.

Question:

Which foods contain starch?

Materials needed:

- •iodine
- •2 small jars
- •eyedropper
- •cornstarch
- •food samples (such as apple, bread, milk, potato, meat, cheese, etc.)
- •small dishes or bowls for food samples

Procedure:

A. Using the eyedropper, put several drops of iodine in a small jar of water. Notice the color of the iodine and water mixture.

B. Mix a teaspoon of cornstarch with water in the other small jar. Add several drops of iodine to this mixture. Notice the color of the iodine, cornstarch, and water mixture.

C. Test some different foods to see if they contain starch by adding several drops of iodine to the food and noting the color. Record your observations in the chart below.

Results:

food	color with iodine	starch	no starch

Conclusions:

1. How do you know if starch is present in the foods you tested? _____
   _____

2. Which of the foods that you tested contain starch? _____
   _____

3. Why does the body need to have starch? _____
   _____

Name _____

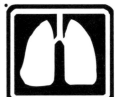

KWL Chart
The Respiratory System

The respiratory system is the system that brings in oxygen from the air and takes away carbon dioxide. Some of the organs of the respiratory system are the nose, trachea, bronchial tubes, lungs, and diaphragm.

Before you begin learning about the respiratory system, complete the first two sections of the chart below. Under **K**, list what you already know about the system. Under **W**, list what you would like to find out about the system. After you have studied the system, go back to the chart and list what you learned under **L**.

K What I know	W What I want to find out	L What I learned

Name _____

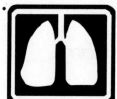

The Respiratory System

The respiratory system is the system of the body that brings in oxygen from the air and takes away carbon dioxide. The body needs to have oxygen to stay alive. **Oxygen** is used by all the cells of the body to help burn food for energy. **Carbon dioxide** is given off as a waste product.

Air comes into the body through the nose (or mouth), and travels into the windpipe, or trachea, which is a tube in the throat. As the **trachea** goes into the chest area, it divides into two branches called **bronchial tubes**, which lead to the lungs. The bronchial tubes branch into smaller and smaller tubes as they enter each lung.

Each of the **lungs** is made up of hundreds of millions of tiny air sacs called **alveoli**. Through these air sacs, oxygen passes into the blood, and carbon dioxide passes out of the blood.

A dome-shaped sheet of muscle under the lungs, called the **diaphragm**, controls breathing in and out. When the diaphragm flattens out, air rushes in to fill up the lungs. This is called **inhaling**. When the diaphragm goes back to its dome shape, it pushes the air back out of the lungs. This is called **exhaling**.

Answer each question.

1. What is the purpose of the respiratory system? _____

   _____

2. What are the parts of the respiratory system? _____

   _____

3. What is the function of the diaphragm? _____

   _____

4. What gas is needed by the body to stay alive? Why? _____

   _____

   _____

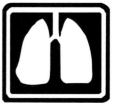

Name _____

Diagram the Respiratory System

Use the number code to label and color the diagram of the respiratory system.

> ## Number Code
> 1. Color the **throat (pharynx)** blue.
> 2. Color the **bronchial tubes** yellow.
> 3. Color the **lungs** orange.
> 4. Color the **nose** and **mouth** red.
> 5. Color the **voice box (larynx)** green.
> 6. Color the **windpipe (trachea)** purple.
> 7. Color the **diaphragm** pink.

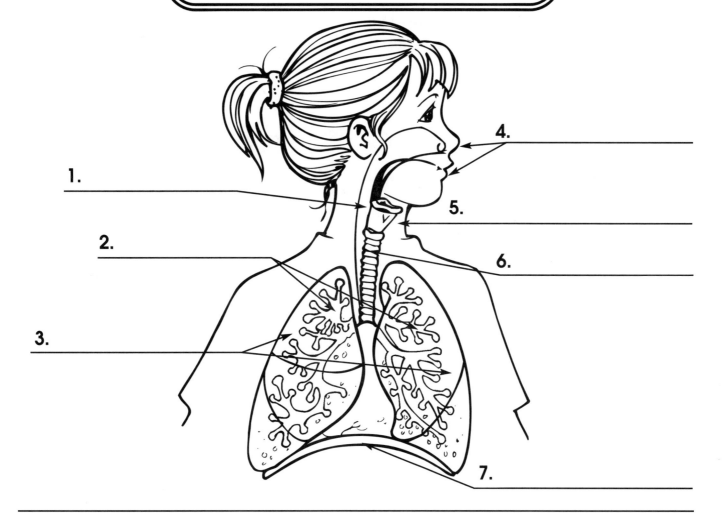

Name _____

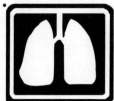

You Take My Breath Away!

Write the letter of each clue about the respiratory system next to the organ or part it describes.

a. You breathe in through me.
   What am I?

b. I am a tube in your throat. I am also called your windpipe.
   What am I?

c. I am one of two branches that lead into your lungs.
   What am I?

d. I am one of two spongy, sac-like organs that absorb oxygen from the air you breath.
   What am I?

e. We are the tiny air sacs in your lungs.
   What are we?

f. I am a dome-shaped sheet of muscle under your lungs that controls breathing in and out.
   What am I?

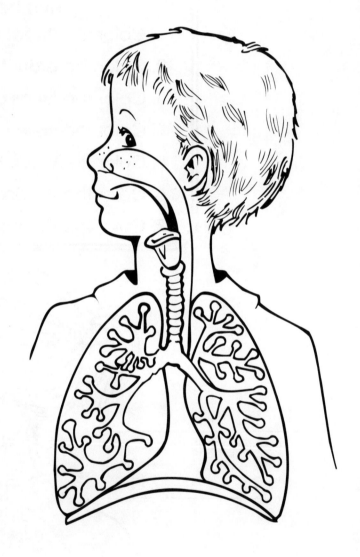

1. _____ diaphragm   2. _____ lung   3. _____ nose

4. _____ trachea   5. _____ alveoli   6. _____ bronchial tube

Name _____

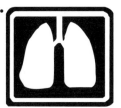

A Breathtaking Experience

Write **T** for true or **F** for false before each statement about the respiratory system. For each statement that is false, rewrite it on another piece of paper to make it a true statement.

_____ 1. The respiratory system brings in oxygen from the air.

_____ 2. The body needs carbon dioxide to survive and gives off oxygen as a waste product.

_____ 3. Air can be breathed in through the nose or the mouth.

_____ 4. The windpipe is another name for the trachea.

_____ 5. The trachea branches into the bronchial tubes.

_____ 6. People have three lungs.

_____ 7. Alveoli are tiny air sacs that make up the lungs.

_____ 8. The diaphragm is a sheet of muscle that controls breathing in and out.

_____ 9. A person inhales when breathing out.

_____ 10. A person exhales when breathing out.

Name _____

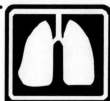

Take a Deep Breath

Use the code to learn some interesting facts about the respiratory system.

Code

A = 1	B = 2	C = 3	D = 4	E = 5	F = 6	G = 7
H = 8	I = 9	J = 10	K = 11	L = 12	M = 13	N = 14
O = 15	P = 16	Q = 17	R = 18	S = 19	T = 20	U = 21
V = 22	W = 23	X = 24	Y = 25	Z = 26		

1. These are found inside of the nose. They help to filter out dirt, fuzz, pollen, or grit that comes in with the air.

$\overline{14}\ \overline{15}\ \overline{19}\ \overline{5}\qquad \overline{8}\ \overline{1}\ \overline{9}\ \overline{18}\ \overline{19}$

2. The nose makes a fresh batch of this every 20 minutes. In one day, the nose makes as much as one quart (.9 liters) of this substance.

$\overline{13}\ \overline{21}\ \overline{3}\ \overline{21}\ \overline{19}$

3. Adults have about 300 million of these in their bodies. They are the air sacs that make up the lungs.

$\overline{1}\ \overline{12}\ \overline{22}\ \overline{5}\ \overline{15}\ \overline{12}\ \overline{9}$

4. At rest, a normal person does this about 10 to 15 times each minute. A baby does this about 40 to 50 times each minute.

$\overline{2}\ \overline{18}\ \overline{5}\ \overline{1}\ \overline{20}\ \overline{8}\ \overline{5}\ \overline{19}$

5. This is exhaled with air when breathing out. It can be seen on a mirror or when breathing out on a really cold day.

$\overline{23}\ \overline{1}\ \overline{20}\ \overline{5}\ \overline{18}\qquad \overline{22}\ \overline{1}\ \overline{16}\ \overline{15}\ \overline{18}$

6. Cases of lung cancer and other lung diseases can be caused by this.

$\overline{19}\ \overline{13}\ \overline{15}\ \overline{11}\ \overline{9}\ \overline{14}\ \overline{7}$

Name _____

Inhale! Exhale!

Match each word or words in List I with its description from List II. Write the number in the box of the matching letter. To discover the magic number, add a row, column, or diagonal. The answer should always be the same!

List I

___ A. respiratory system

___ B. nose

___ C. trachea

___ D. bronchial tubes

___ E. lungs

___ F. diaphragm

___ G. alveoli

___ H. inhale

___ I. exhale

A.	B.	C.
D.	E.	F.
G.	H.	I.

List II

2. to breathe in

3. a tube in the throat that is also called the windpipe

4. two short, wide tubes that connect the trachea to the lungs

5. the system that controls the exchange of oxygen and carbon dioxide in the body

6. two spongy, sac-like organs that are used for breathing

7. to breathe out

8. strong wall of muscle under the lungs that controls breathing in and out

9. tiny air sacs in the lungs that let oxygen pass into the blood and help carbon dioxide to leave the blood

10. part of the body that is used to breathe in

Magic Number _____

Name _____

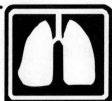

A Breath of Fresh Air

Circle the words from the Word Bank in the puzzle. The words appear horizontally, vertically, and diagonally.

Word Bank

alveoli	exhale	oxygen	breathe
inhale	lungs	trachea	windpipe
carbon dioxide	mouth	diaphragm	nose
respiratory system	bronchial tubes		

```
r  r  o  z  c  h  b  a  t  x  k  b  y  s
e  b  n  o  x  y  g  e  n  v  s  o  e  r
s  r  o  s  l  m  p  m  g  g  t  x  t  e
p  o  d  d  u  o  o  n  n  w  r  g  r  c
i  n  o  i  g  u  u  u  i  i  e  e  a  t
r  c  a  e  a  t  l  t  t  n  a  r  c  h
a  h  i  r  c  p  f  h  h  h  b  m  h  e
t  i  n  n  b  r  h  e  o  o  r  o  e  e
o  a  h  i  d  o  e  r  n  s  e  t  a  x
r  l  a  s  o  e  n  d  a  y  a  h  e  h
y  t  l  e  o  r  i  d  g  g  t  l  x  b
s  u  e  n  n  o  s  e  i  t  m  u  h  r
y  b  w  e  x  h  a  l  e  o  v  n  i  e
s  e  d  i  u  v  o  u  l  r  x  n  n  a
t  s  d  w  i  n  d  p  i  p  e  i  e  t
e  e  a  l  v  e  o  l  i  d  y  g  d  h
m  w  x  k  l  k  c  i  a  i  t  s  u  e
```

Name _____

Catch Your Breath!

Use the words from the Word Bank to complete the crossword puzzle.

Down

1. the windpipe in the throat where air enters after it comes into the nose or mouth

3. the waste product given off when exhaling

4. breathing in, or air coming into the lungs

5. the two organs that air passes into and out of so blood can receive oxygen and give off carbon dioxide

6. breathing out, or pushing air out of the lungs

8. the gas in the air that is needed by the body to burn food energy to stay alive

Word Bank

oxygen	lungs
trachea	nose
exhaling	alveoli
bronchial tubes	
diaphragm	
inhaling	
carbon dioxide	

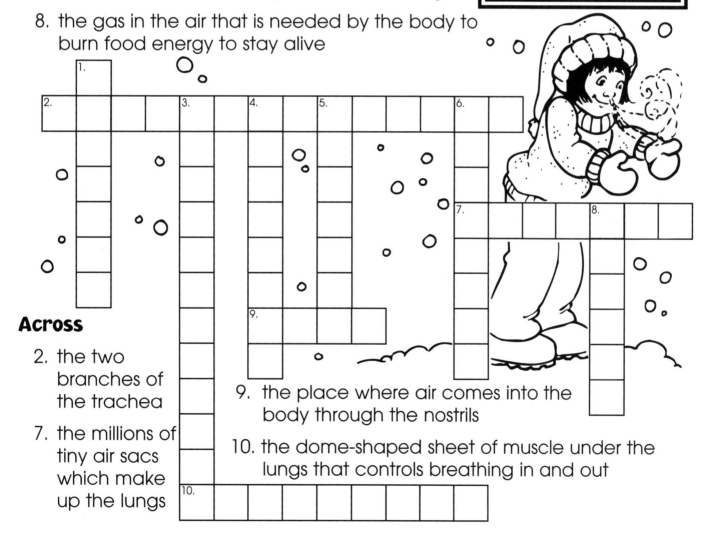

Across

2. the two branches of the trachea

7. the millions of tiny air sacs which make up the lungs

9. the place where air comes into the body through the nostrils

10. the dome-shaped sheet of muscle under the lungs that controls breathing in and out

Name _____

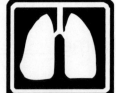

Full of Hot Air

Question:
What is the amount of air that your lungs can hold when you take a deep breath?

Materials Needed:
- large jug (about 1 gallon) • water   • plastic straw
- rubber or plastic tubing   • large bucket or dishpan
- graduated cylinder or measuring cup

Procedure:

A. Fill the jug to the top with water.

B. Fill the dishpan or bucket about one fourth of the way full.

C. Use one hand to cover the mouth of the jug as you turn it upside down into the water.

D. Put one end of the tubing into the jug after it is upside down.

E. Put a piece of plastic straw into the other end of the tubing. This is the end that you will use to blow into the jug.

F. Take a deep breath. Then put your mouth on the straw and blow into it until you have blown out all of the air in your lungs.

G. Slide your hand over the mouth of the jug and turn it right side up with out letting any water escape.

H. Use the measuring cup or graduated cylinder to measure the amount of water that it takes to refill the jug. The amount of air you exhaled is equal to the amount of water you used to refill the jug.

Results:
What is the amount of air that your lungs held? _____

Conclusions:
Do you think adults can hold more air in their lungs than children? How could you find out? What other things might have an effect on how much air your lungs can hold? _____

_____

_____

Name _____

A Model of a Lung

Below the lungs is a sheet of muscle called the diaphragm. Because the lungs are not muscles, they cannot move by themselves to bring air in and out. In this activity, you will create a model of a lung to show what happens to the diaphragm as you breathe.

Question:

How do the diaphragm and lungs work together in breathing?

Materials Needed: •clear plastic bottle (two-liter size)   •scissors
• two large 12-inch balloons •masking tape •rubber band

Procedure:

A. Soak and peel the label off the bottle. Then cut off the bottom half of the bottle and put masking tape along the cut edge.

B. Put one of the balloons into the mouth of the bottle, stretching the mouth of the balloon over the top of the bottle. This balloon shows how your lung behaves.

C. Cut off the top of the other balloon and stretch it over the bottom of the bottle, using the rubber band to hold it in place. This balloon shows how your diaphragm behaves.

D. Pull outward on the balloon on the bottom of the bottle using your fore finger and thumb. Observe what happens to the balloon on the inside of the bottle. Let go of the bottom balloon so that it returns to its original position. Again, observe what happens to the balloon inside the bottle.

Results:

Describe what happened to the balloon inside the bottle when you pulled outward on the other balloon and when you let go of it.

Conclusions:

1. Tell what part of your respiratory system the bottom balloon is like and what part the top balloon is like. _____

2. How do the diaphragm and lungs work together in breathing? _____

_____

     Human Body: Grades 2–3

Name _____

KWL Chart
The Circulatory System

The circulatory system is the system that carries materials throughout the body. Some of the main parts of the circulatory system are the heart, arteries, veins, capillaries, and blood.

Before you begin learning about the circulatory system, complete the first two sections of the chart below. Under **K**, list what you already know about the system. Under **W**, list what you would like to find out about the system. After you have studied the system, go back to the chart and list what you learned under **L**.

K What I know	W What I want to find out	L What I learned

Name _____

The Circulatory System

The function of the circulatory system is to carry materials all through the body. The main parts of the circulatory system are the **heart**, the **blood vessels**, and the **blood**. Blood carries food and oxygen to all the cells of the body as it is pumped through the blood vessels by the heart. The circulatory system also helps carry away waste products such as carbon dioxide.

The heart is a very hardworking pump that is made up of muscle cells. It has two upper chambers, or hollow areas, called **atria**, and two lower chambers called **ventricles**. The atrium and the ventricle on the left side of the heart receive the oxygen-rich blood from the lungs and carry it to all parts of the body. The atrium and ventricle on the right side receive the oxygen-poor blood from the body and send it to the lungs where it can get rid of the carbon dioxide and receive oxygen. Then, the whole cycle can repeat itself.

There are three main types of blood vessels. The largest blood vessels are the **arteries** which carry the blood away from the heart. The arteries branch into smaller and smaller blood vessels until they are so tiny that only one cell at a time can pass through them. These tiny blood vessels are called **capillaries**. The capillaries join together into larger blood vessels called **veins** which carry the blood back to the heart.

The liquid part of the blood is called **plasma**. It makes up a little over half of the blood. The rest of the blood is made up of different kinds of solid particles such as **red blood cells, white blood cells**, and **platelets**. The red blood cells carry the oxygen and the carbon dioxide in the body. The white blood cells help the body attack germs and fight diseases. The platelets help the blood to form a clot to seal an injury to a blood vessel when there is a cut or wound.

Answer each question.

1. What is the purpose of the circulatory system? _____

   _____

2. What are the three main types of blood vessels? _____

   _____

3. What are the main parts of the circulatory system? _____

   _____

4. What are some of the solid particles that make up the blood? _____

   _____

Name _____

The Heart of the Matter

Match the beginning of each sentence to its correct ending. Write the letter of each ending on the line before each beginning. Then label the diagram of the four chambers of the heart. They are the left atrium, left ventricle, right atrium, and right ventricle.

_____ **1.** When the heart beats,

_____ **2.** When the heart relaxes,

_____ **3.** Each side of the heart

_____ **4.** The left ventricle

_____ **5.** The right atrium

_____ **6.** The right ventricle

_____ **7.** The left atrium

a. it allows blood to flow into it from the body.

b. it pumps blood through blood vessels throughout the body.

c. receives oxygen-rich blood from the lungs.

d. has an atrium and a ventricle.

e. receives the blood from the body that needs oxygen.

f. pumps the oxygen-rich blood through the aorta out to the body.

g. pumps the blood to the lungs.

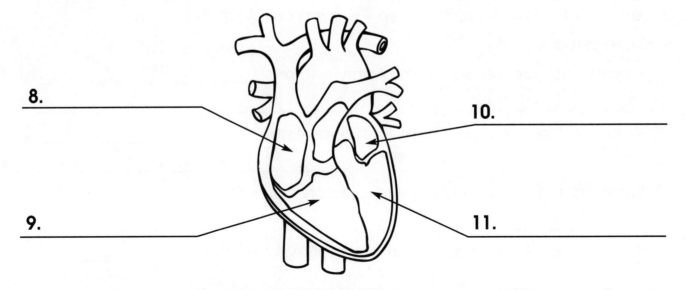

8. _____

9. _____

10. _____

11. _____

Name _____

Getting Carried Away

Blood is pumped by the heart to all parts of the body through tubes called **blood vessels**. Blood is made up of red blood cells, white blood cells, platelets, and plasma. **Red blood cells** are disc-shaped and carry oxygen to all parts of the body. **White blood cells** attack germs and fight diseases. **Platelets** are needed for blood to clot, so that a cut stops bleeding. **Plasma** is the liquid part of the blood. Plasma is made mostly of water.

In the diagram below, color the red blood cells red. Color the white blood cells orange. Color the platelets pink. Color the plasma yellow.

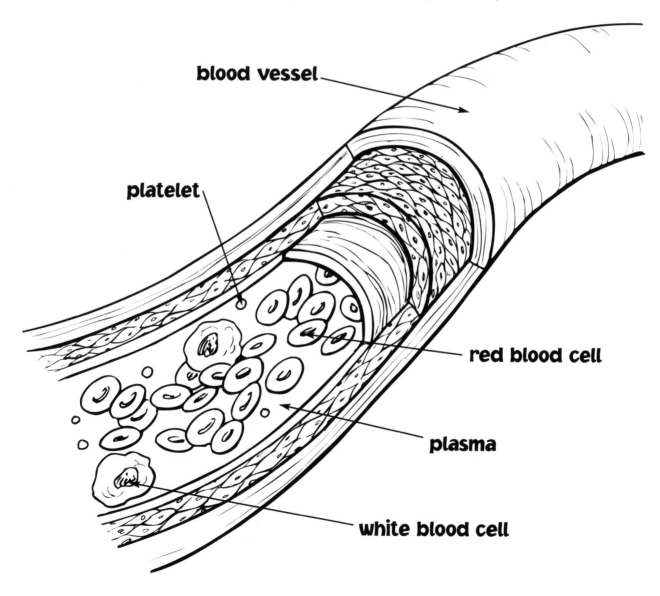

Name _____

Go with the Flow

Write **T** for true or **F** for false before each statement about the circulatory system. For each statement that is false, rewrite it on another piece of paper to make it a true statement.

_____ 1. The circulatory system carries blood throughout the body.

_____ 2. The heart, blood, and blood vessels make up the circulatory system.

_____ 3. The heart is not a muscle.

_____ 4. There are four chambers in the heart.

_____ 5. Arteries, veins, and capillaries are all types of blood vessels.

_____ 6. Arteries, veins, and capillaries are all the same size.

_____ 7. The liquid part of the blood is called plasma.

_____ 8. Red blood cells help the body attack germs and fight disease.

_____ 9. White blood cells carry the oxygen in the body.

_____ 10. Platelets help blood to clot.

Name _____

All About the Circulatory System

Use the code to learn some interesting facts about the circulatory system.

Code

A=1	B=2	C=3	D=4	E=5	F=6	G=7
H=8	I=9	J=10	K=11	L=12	M=13	N=14
O=15	P=16	Q=17	R=18	S=19	T=20	U=21
V=22	W=23	X=24	Y=25	Z=26		

1. This sound is caused by the muscles in the heart and the closing of valves in the heart which keep the blood from flowing backward.

   ___ ___ ___ ___ ___ ___ ___ ___ ___
   8   5   1   18   20   2   5   1   20

2. This is what it feels like when blood has not been circulating very well through your hands and feet and then you begin to move them.

   ___ ___ ___ ___ and ___ ___ ___ ___ ___ ___ ___
   16   9   14   19   14   5   5   4   12   5   19

3. The heart is shaped more like this fruit than like the hearts on Valentine's Day cards.

   ___ ___ ___ ___
   16   5   1   18

4. It has been estimated that, if you laid them end to end, these would circle the globe twice over.

   ___ ___ ___ ___ ___   ___ ___ ___ ___ ___ ___ ___
   2   12 15 15   4   22   5   19   19   5   12 19

5. When the body has an infection, blood has an extra amount of these in it.

   ___ ___ ___ ___ ___   ___ ___ ___ ___ ___   ___ ___ ___ ___ ___
   23   8   9   20   5   2   12 15 15   4   3   5   12 12 19

6. In an adult, this organ beats about 70 times per minute, or about 105,000 times per day. Each day, it pumps 1,800 gallons (6,813 liters) of blood through 60,000 miles of blood vessels (560.6 kilometers).

   ___ ___ ___ ___ ___
   8   5   1   18   20

Name _____

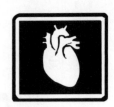

Follow the Flow

Circle the words from the Word Bank in the puzzle. The words appear horizontally, vertically, diagonally, and backwards.

Word Bank

arteries	circulatory system	red blood cells
heart	blood vessels	white blood cells
blood	plasma	ventricles
platelets	capillaries	atrium veins

```
c  a  b  a  p  i  l  l  a  r  c  e  s
i  b  l  l  a  b  d  c  w  v  i  v  p
r  x  o  s  o  t  y  b  h  e  c  l  l
c  y  o  h  b  o  u  l  i  n  a  v  a
u  z  d  a  e  e  d  o  t  t  r  c  s
l  a  v  r  f  a  s  o  e  r  o  a  m
a  b  e  t  g  j  r  l  b  i  y  p  a
t  v  s  o  o  k  e  t  l  c  s  i  x
o  e  s  n  i  t  i  s  o  l  y  l  y
r  n  e  s  s  d  n  t  o  e  s  l  a
y  t  l  m  n  i  i  d  d  s  t  a  r
s  c  s  n  e  e  i  v  c  w  e  r  t
y  e  o  v  v  l  l  e  e  x  m  i  e
s  l  l  e  c  d  o  o  l  b  d  e  r
t  l  s  b  l  o  o  b  l  x  v  s  i
e  x  s  v  e  n  s  v  s  y  e  x  e
m  d  e  r  m  u  i  r  t  a  s  a  s
```

Name _____

Merrily We Flow Along

The sentences below are not in order. Number the sentences in order to tell the path that a drop of blood would follow through the circulatory system. The first sentence has been identified.

_____ Oxygen-poor blood passes from the right atrium to the right ventricle of the heart.

__1__ Oxygen-rich blood is pumped from the left ventricle of the heart into the aorta, or main artery, which branches into smaller arteries.

_____ The oxygen-poor blood goes into the veins and to the right atrium of the heart.

_____ From the right ventricle, oxygen-poor blood is pumped to the lungs where it gives off carbon dioxide and picks up oxygen.

_____ From the aorta, oxygen-rich blood is carried from the arteries to the capillaries all throughout the body.

_____ After it picks up oxygen in the lungs, the now oxygen-rich blood is carried from the lungs to the left atrium. Oxygen-rich blood passes from the left atrium into the left ventricle.

_____ In the capillaries, the blood gives oxygen to the cells and picks up carbon dioxide, so the blood is now oxygen-poor.

This cycle of blood flow repeats over and over throughout your lifetime!

Name _____

Your Beating Heart

The heart is a muscle that pumps the blood through tubes, or blood vessels, inside the body. Every time the heart beats, the arteries swell a small amount as the blood pushes through. This is called the pulse. The pulse in the wrist or in the side of the neck can be felt by lightly holding the forefinger and middle finger on one of these spots.

> **Question:**
> Will exercise have an effect on your pulse rate?

Materials Needed: a clock or a watch with a second hand

Procedure:

A. Sit quietly for a few minutes. Predict and write down how many times you think your heart will beat in one minute.

B. Find your pulse in your wrist or neck. Count the number of times you can feel your pulse in one minute. Write this down. (For a faster method, count how many times you can feel your pulse in ten seconds. Multiply this number by six to find out how many times your heart beats in one minute, which is 60 seconds.)

C. Run in place or go up and down some stairs for one minute. Count and write down your pulse after you have exercised. Repeat the activity for seven minutes.

Results:

I predict that my pulse rate when I am sitting quietly (resting) will be _____ beats per minute. My actual pulse rate while resting was _____ beats per minute.

pulse (beats per minute) after exercise

minutes	1	2	3	4	5	6	7

Conclusions:

How did your pulse rate change after you exercised? _____

Why did this happen?_____

How long did it take for your pulse to go back to normal? Did your pulse rate go back down as quickly as it went up? Explain. _____
_____

Name _____

KWL Chart
The Nervous System

The nervous system is the system that receives and carries messages to control the body, and coordinates all of the body systems. Some of the main parts of the nervous system are the brain, the spinal cord, and the nerves.

Before you begin learning about the nervous system, complete the first two sections of the chart below. Under **K**, list what you already know about the system. Under **W**, list what you would like to find out about the system. After you have studied the system, go back to the chart and list what you learned under **L**.

K What I know	W What I want to find out	L What I learned

Name _____

The Nervous System

The **nervous system** is the system of the body that receives and carries messages all throughout the body. The nervous system controls and coordinates all the body parts. The main organs of the nervous system are the brain, the spinal cord, and the nerves. These organs are made of special nerve cells called **neurons**.

Together, the brain and spinal cord make up what is called the **central nervous system**. They work together to analyze and store information that comes in from outside the body, and they to pass on instructions to the other body parts about how to respond. The **brain** has three main parts: the **cerebrum**, the **cerebellum**, and the **medulla**. The cerebrum is the largest part of the brain, and it controls all learning, memory, and reasoning. It controls many body parts. It is made up of a right half and a left half, and each half controls the opposite half of the body. The cerebellum is below the cerebrum. It is the part of the brain that controls balance and coordination. The medulla is the part of the brain that controls body actions such as heartbeat, sneezing, and coughing. These are called **involuntary** actions because they are not consciously controlled.

The **peripheral nervous system** is the network of neurons, or nerve cells, that spread out from the spinal cord to the rest of the body. These **nerves** carry messages between the central nervous system and all the other parts of the body. Sense organs such as the eyes, ears, nose, and skin bring in messages to the brain about conditions outside of the body.

Answer each question.

1. What is the purpose of the nervous system? _____

_____

2. What are the main organs of the nervous system? _____

_____

3. What are the three main parts of the brain and what do they control? _____

_____

_____

_____

Name _____

A Bundle of nerves

The nervous system is made up of the central nervous system and the peripheral nervous system.

Follow the directions below to label the brain, spinal cord, and nerves.

1. The **brain** is located at the top of the spinal cord. Label the brain.

2. The **spinal cord** is a bundle of nerves inside the spinal column. Label the spinal cord.

3. The **nerves** spread out from the spinal cord to the rest of the body. Label the nerves.

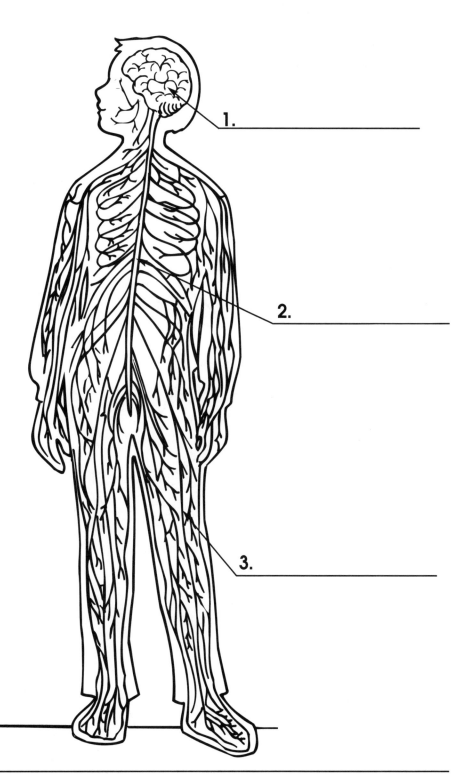

1. _____

2. _____

3. _____

Name _____

Brain Power

The central nervous system is made up of the brain and spinal cord.

Use the number code to label and color the diagram of the brain.

> ### Number Code
> 1. Color the **cerebrum** red.
> 2. Color the **cerebellum** blue.
> 3. Color the **spinal cord** green.
> 4. Color the **medulla** yellow.

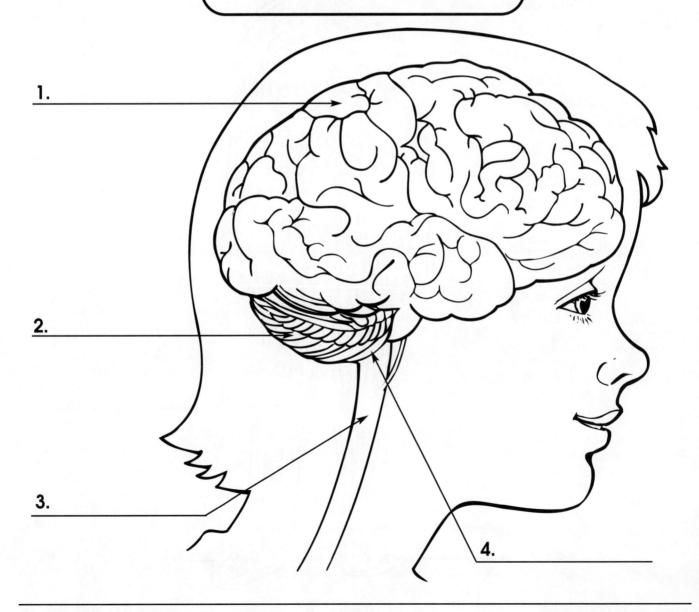

Name _____

True or False?

Write **T** for true or **F** for false before each statement about the nervous system. For each statement that is false, rewrite it on another piece of paper to make it a true statement.

_____ 1. The nervous system controls all of the body parts.

_____ 2. The brain and spinal cord make up the central nervous system.

_____ 3. The parts of the brain are the cerebrum, the cerebellum, and the medulla.

_____ 4. The cerebellum is the largest part of the brain.

_____ 5. The cerebrum controls balance and coordination.

_____ 6. The medulla controls body actions like heartbeat and coughing.

_____ 7. The peripheral nervous system and the central nervous system are the same thing.

_____ 8. Neurons are nerve cells that carry messages to other parts of the body.

Name _____

All About the Nervous System

Use the code to learn some interesting facts about the nervous system.

Code

A = 1	B = 2	C = 3	D = 4	E = 5	F = 6	G = 7
H = 8	I = 9	J = 10	K = 11	L = 12	M = 13	N = 14
O = 15	P = 16	Q = 17	R = 18	S = 19	T = 20	U = 21
V = 22	W = 23	X = 24	Y = 25	Z = 26		

1. This organ carries information between the brain and the rest of the body. It stops growing when children are about four to five years old. In adults, it is about 17 inches (43 cm) long and 0.8 inches (2 cm.) thick.

    ___ ___ ___ ___ ___ ___   ___ ___ ___ ___
    19 16 9   14 1   12   3   15 18 4

2. The brain is made up of these. One of these in the brain can connect to 25,000 others.

    ___ ___ ___ ___ ___
    3   5   12 12 19

3. If you took all of these from the body and laid them end to end, they would measure about 47 miles (75 km).

    ___ ___ ___ ___ ___ ___
    14 5   18 22 5   19

4. These are carried and sent by nerves. They can travel over 249 miles (400 km) per hour. They travel as electrical impulses.

    ___ ___ ___ ___ ___ ___ ___
    19 9   7   14 1   12 19

5. This organ weighs about three pounds and is a little larger than a grapefruit. It is the most complex organ in the body, and it controls all activities.

    ___ ___ ___ ___ ___
    2   18 1   9   14

Name _____

It Takes Brains

Circle the words from the Word Bank to solve the puzzle. The words appear horizontally, vertically, and diagonally.

Word Bank

central nervous system	brain	medulla	neurons
peripheral nerves	cerebrum	nerves	spinal cord
nervous system	cerebellum		

```
c  u  l  l  a  x  b  h  y  z  e  a  c
o  s  y  s  n  e  r  v  e  s  s  p  e
r  n  p  a  b  c  v  e  r  n  e  e  n
d  i  a  i  r  s  c  i  n  m  l  r  t
c  m  b  u  n  e  e  u  u  n  l  i  r
h  e  c  m  t  a  l  l  e  r  u  p  a
u  d  r  s  e  d  l  s  e  l  d  h  l
r  u  h  e  m  e  n  c  n  a  e  e  n
b  l  i  i  b  l  e  r  o  r  m  r  e
e  l  g  e  r  r  a  u  r  u  a  r  r
r  a  r  r  a  l  u  i  r  e  d  l  v
e  e  o  o  i  a  v  m  o  c  h  n  o
c  l  h  c  e  n  t  r  a  l  n  e  u
e  m  p  h  o  s  e  r  s  p  n  r  s
r  n  e  u  r  o  n  s  s  e  e  v  s
e  q  u  x  z  i  o  p  r  s  w  e  y
u  r  v  s  a  g  b  r  i  n  s  s  y
l  s  w  r  a  c  d  i  g  t  m  e  t
l  t  b  t  b  o  u  s  s  y  s  t  e
n  e  r  v  o  u  s  s  y  s  t  e  m
```

Name _____

Getting on Your Nerves

Use the Word Bank to complete the crossword puzzle.

Word Bank

spinal cord
medulla
central
cerebrum
cerebellum
nerves
neurons
brain
peripheral

Across

1. the largest part of the brain; controls learning, memory, and reasoning

3. messages are sent by the brain through this out to all the other nerves in the body; protected by the spine

7. the control center of the body located in the head

9. the part of the brain that is below the cerebrum; controls balance and coordination

Down

2. the part of the brain that controls automatic actions such as sneezing

4. the nervous system that is made up of the network of nerves that spread out all over the body from the spinal cord

5. what carries the signals to and from the brain

6. the nervous system that is made up of the brain and spinal cord

8. another name for nerve cells

74

Name _____

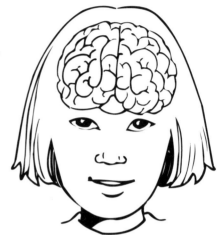

Which Is Your Dominant Side?

Every movement of the body is controlled by the two sides of the brain. The left side of the brain controls the right side of the body, and the right side of the brain controls the left side of the body. Most people have a favorite hand that they use to do things, but many people are not totally left-handed or right-handed. Use the following activities to try and find out which side of your brain is stronger, or more dominant.

Put an X in the box for the hand, foot, ear, or eye that you use for each activity.

activity	right	left
Blink one of your eyes.		
Pick up a spoon or fork to eat.		
Hop on one foot.		
Write your name.		
Throw a ball.		
Look through a microscope or hole.		
Listen to a soft noise.		
Kick a ball.		
Use scissors.		

How many boxes did you mark for left? _____

How many boxes did you mark for right? _____

Remember, the right side of your brain controls the left side of your body and vice versa. Which side of your brain seems to be the dominant side?

_____

Name _____

How Fast Can You React?

Have you ever had someone say "think fast" and throw a ball at you? In order for your body to react and catch the ball, several things must happen. Your ears and eyes send messages to the brain. Your brain figures out the messages and sends messages back out to your muscles to react. The amount of time that this takes is called your reaction time.

> **Question:**
> How long does it take for your brain to receive a message and react to it?

Materials: ruler

Procedures:

A. Have a partner hold a ruler above your hand at the end with the highest marking (12 inches or 30 cm).

B. Hold your thumb and first finger about 5 cm (2 inches) apart, close to, but not touching, the bottom of the ruler.

C. As your partner lets go of the ruler, try to catch it as quickly as possible using only your thumb and first finger. Write down how far the ruler dropped before you caught it. The lower the number, the faster your reaction time.

D. Repeat this experiment two more times and write down your results.

E. Repeat the entire procedure using your left hand to catch the ruler and write down the results.

Results:

	reaction time distance (ruler)	
	right hand	left hand
1.		
2.		
3.		

Conclusions:

Did your reaction time get better as you repeated the experiment? _____

Is there a difference in reaction time between your right hand and your left hand? Explain. _____

_____

How do you think an older person's reaction time would compare to the reaction time of someone your age? Why?_____

Name _____

KWL Chart
The Five Senses

Before you begin learning about the five senses, hearing, seeing, smelling, touching, and tasting, complete the first two sections of the chart below.

Under **K**, list what you already know about the senses. Under **W**, list what you would like to find out about the senses. After you have studied the senses, go back to the chart and list what you learned under **L**.

K What I know	W What I want to find out	L What I learned

Name _____

Sight-Seeing

The **eye** is the organ used for the sense of sight. The eyes contain special cells that can detect light. The front part of the eye is the **cornea**. Light enters the eye through a small opening called the **pupil**. The **iris**, which is the colored part of the eye, controls how much light comes through the pupil. When light enters the eye, it goes through a **lens**. The lens is the clear part of the eye that bends light, forming a small picture on the back wall of the eye. This back wall is called the **retina**. The retina has millions of cells that are close to nerve endings. Light hits the cells, and nerve endings pick up messages. These messages then travel along the **optic nerve** to the brain where they are interpreted. The brain then "tells" you what you see.

Answer each question.

1. What is the cornea? _____

_____

2. What is the pupil? _____

_____

3. What is the iris, and what does the iris do? _____

_____

_____

4. What is the lens? _____

_____

5. What is the retina, and what happens in the retina? _____

_____

Name _____

Seeing Is Believing

Use the number code to label and color the diagram of the eye.

Number Code

1. Color the **cornea** purple.
2. Color the **pupil** black.
3. Color the **iris** blue.
4. Color the **lens** yellow.
5. Color the **retina** orange.
6. Color the **nerve** that leads to the brain red.

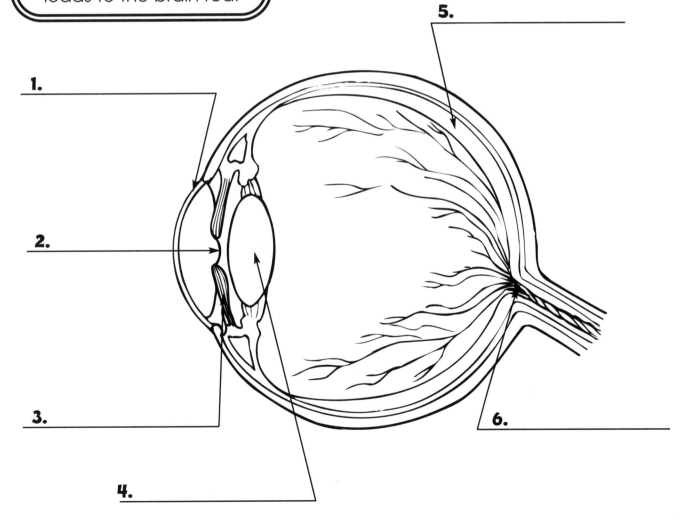

1.

2.

3.

4.

5.

6.

Name _____

What Am I?

Each of these clues tells something about the eyes or the sense of sight. Choose a word from the Word Bank to answer each question.

Word Bank

cornea   pupil   eye   iris   lens   retina   optic nerve

1. I am the organ used for seeing.

   What am I? _____

2. I am the clear, front part of the eye.

   What am I? _____

3. I am the colored part of the eye.

   What am I? _____

4. I am the round, dark opening in the center of the iris. My job is to control the amount of light entering the eye.

   What am I? _____

5. I am the clear part of the eye that focuses light on the retina.

   What am I? _____

6. I am the back wall of the eye. I receive light images from the lens.

   What am I? _____

7. I am a special nerve that carries messages from the eyes to the brain.

   What am I? _____

Name _____

Seeing Eye to Eye

Complete the crossword puzzle.

Across

2. the nerve that carries messages to the brain

4. the back wall of the eye

7. organ used for seeing

Down

1. small opening through which light enters the eye

3. the clear, front part of the eye

5. the colored part of the eye

6. clear part of the eye that focuses light

Name _____

The Eyes Have It

Circle the words from the Word Bank in the puzzle. The words appear horizontally, vertically, diagonally, and backwards.

Word Bank

blink	eye	eyelid	lens
pupil	sight	vision	cornea
iris	nerve	eyelash	retina

```
e  e  t  r  r  e  t  i  n  a  s
y  y  n  e  y  t  e  s  d  e
v  l  e  t  e  h  f  v  l  k
i  i  r  l  i  g  k  e  s  n
s  d  v  i  a  i  n  l  e  i
i  p  e  s  d  s  d  m  n  l
o  u  i  g  a  p  h  p  r  b
n  r  h  h  s  p  u  p  i  l  c
i  n  c  o  r  n  e  a  t  c
s  k  d  i  l  e  y  e  s  e
```

Name _____

The Hole Story

Each of the eyes focuses on an image that the brain puts together into one picture. This allows you to judge distances and to see things in three dimensions. In this experiment, you will try to find out what happens when your eyes are focusing on images at two different distances.

> **Question:**
> How does your brain put the images from each of your eyes into one picture?

Materials: one sheet of paper

Procedure:

A. Roll the sheet of paper into a long tube.

B. Hold the tube up to one eye and close the other eye.

C. Put your other hand alongside of the tube with your palm toward your face.

D. Open your other eye so that both eyes are open and observe the appearance of your hand.

Results:

What did you notice when you looked at your hand with one eye and through the tube with your other eye? _____

_____

Draw a picture of what your hand looked like when you viewed it this way.

Conclusions:

What you observed is called an **optical illusion**. Read the first sentence at the top of this page and explain in your own words why it looked like you had a hole in your hand. _____

_____

Name _____

Don't Be So Blind

The optic nerve is the nerve that carries the messages from each of the eyes to the brain. The eye has a spot from where the optic nerve leaves. This is called the "blind spot" because, at this spot, things cannot be seen at a certain distance. In this experiment, you will try to find your blind spot.

Question:
Where is the blind spot in your eye?

Materials: •paper •pencil •ruler

Procedure:

A. Draw an O about the size of a dime in the middle of the piece of paper.

B. Draw an X about 7.25 inches to the right of the O.

C. Hold the paper out in front of you at arm's length and close your left eye. Slowly move the paper toward you while staring at the O and observe what happens to the X.

D. Hold the paper out in front of you at arm's length again, this time closing your right eye. Stare at the X as you move the paper toward you and observe what happens to the O.

Results:

Tell what happened to the X as you stared at the O while moving the paper toward you. _____

Tell what happened to the O as you stared at the X while moving the paper toward you. _____

Conclusions:

Why do you think the X and the O seem to disappear when you look at them from a certain distance? _____

_____

Do you think the distance at which they seem to disappear is the same for each eye? _____

Name _____

The Ears and Hearing

The **ear** is made up of three parts: the outer ear, the middle ear, and the inner ear. The part of the ear that can be seen is the **outer ear**. The outer ear catches sound waves and sends them into the **ear canal**. Vibrating air in the ear canal makes the **eardrum** vibrate. The eardrum is a thin sheet of tissue at the end of the ear canal. These vibrations pass from the eardrum through three small bones that make up the **middle ear**. These small bones (the smallest bones in the body) are called the **hammer**, the **anvil**, and the **stirrup**. They pass the vibrations on to the inner ear. A long, coiled tube that looks like a snail's shell is in the **inner ear**. It is called the **cochlea**. As vibrations cause the liquid in the cochlea to move, tiny hair-like nerve endings in the cochlea also move. The nerve endings send signals to the brain, and the sound is heard.

Answer each question.

1. What are the names of the three parts of the ear? _____

_____

2. What is the eardrum, and where is it located? _____

_____

3. What are the names of the three small bones that make up the middle ear? _____

_____

4. What happens in the inner ear? _____

_____

_____

Name _____

Do You Hear What I Hear?

Use the number code to label and color the diagram of the ear.

Number Code

1. Color the **outer ear** brown.
2. Color the **ear canal** yellow.
3. Color the **eardrum** blue.
4. Color the **middle ear** green.
5. Color the **inner ear** red.

Who wants ice cream?

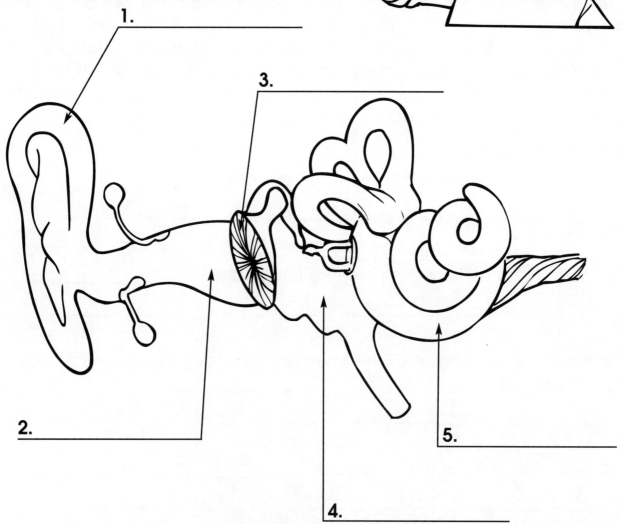

1.

2.

3.

4.

5.

Name _____

Do You Hear Me?

Each of the following clues tells something about the ears and the sense of hearing. Use the words from the Word Bank to answer the questions.

Word Bank

cochlea	ear	middle ear
outer ear	ear canal	eardrum

1. I am the organ used for hearing. I also help people maintain balance.

   What am I? _____

2. I am the part of the ear you can see.

   What am I? _____

3. I am a short, tubular pathway in the ear. Sound travels from the outer ear, through me, then into the eardrum.

   What am I? _____

4. I am a thin sheet of tissue at the end of the ear canal. Sound passes through me to the middle ear.

   What am I? _____

5. I am the part of the ear that contains the hammer, anvil, and stirrup.

   What am I? _____

6. I am a coiled, fluid-filled tube found in the inner ear.

   What am I? _____

Name _____

All Ears

Unscramble the words to find the answers to the clues about the ears and the sense of hearing. Use the numbered letters to find the answers to the riddles below.

1. the part of the ear you can see

    troeeura   __ __ __ __ __ __ __ __
                       3   2

2. thin tissue at the end of the ear canal

    dermuar   __ __ __ __ __ __ __
                           1   4

3. one of the three small bones in the middle ear

    rristpu   __ __ __ __ __ __ __
                     5   8

4. short, tubular pathway that sound travels through

    cnlaarea   __ __ __   __ __ __ __
                                 6

5. a coiled, fluid-filled tube in the inner ear

    acolche   __ __ __ __ __ __ __
                        7

6. organ used for hearing

    era   __ __ __
                 9

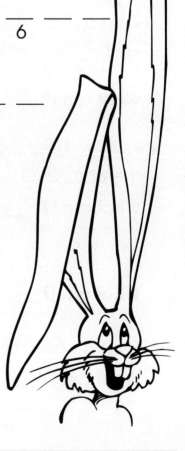

What instruments did the rock star carry in his ears?

        __ __ __ __ __
        1 2 3 4 5

What pierces your ears without leaving a hole?

        __ __ __ __ __
        6 7 8 5 9

Human Body: Grades 2–3

Name _____

Hear All About It!

Complete the crossword puzzle.

Across

1. the part of the ear you see

4. the part of the ear that contains the hammer, anvil, and stirrup

6. a coiled, fluid-filled tube in the inner ear

Down

2. a thin tissue at the end of the ear canal

3. short, tubular pathway that sound travels through

5. organ used for hearing

Name _____

Sense of Hearing

Circle the words from the Word Bank in the puzzle. The words appear horizontally, vertically, diagonally, and backwards.

Word Bank

anvil	ear canal	eardrum	hear
sound	cochlea	middle ear	earwax
inner ear	ear		

```
c i c g j p v v e a c v d s
a q l w r b e a n u d c a t
j e h e n q r v v r j o z i
g p r m u c i l l k v y n x
x z q a a l g c o c h l e a
z c b n e i s i i c g y p w
t l a r k e n o h g v r c r
g l a j w s l n u c d h g a
z e t f i w m d e n i t c e
h q k i d c w t d r d l w a
a d c w e a r c s i e v z w
s m o l e z b f v e m a i a
p n m u r d r a e m a h r x
```

Name _____

Taste and Smell

The senses of taste and smell are closely related. The sense of smell helps when tasting food.

When breathing, the **nose** takes in air that carries odors. These odors enter the **nostrils** and travel to the **nasal cavities**, which are lined with mucus. There, nerve endings pick up odors and send messages to the brain, which let the brain know what it is smelling.

There are about 10,000 **taste buds** covering the surface of the **tongue**. Taste buds are made up of cells that are connected to nerve endings. The tastes of different foods are picked up by these nerve cells. At the tip of the tongue are the taste buds for sensing sweet tastes like chocolate. A little farther back and on the sides of the tongue are the taste buds for tasting salty foods like potato chips. Sour foods can be sensed by the taste buds on the far back sides of the tongue and on the roof of the mouth. At the very back of the tongue is where foods that taste bitter are sensed.

Answer each question.

1. How does the nose detect odors in the air? _____
_____

2. What are taste buds? How many taste buds does the tongue have?
_____
_____

3. What are the four tastes that taste buds can detect, and where are each of these located on the tongue? _____
_____
_____
_____

Name _____

Want a Taste?

This diagram of the tongue shows the areas where different kinds of taste buds are located.

List three foods for each kind of taste.

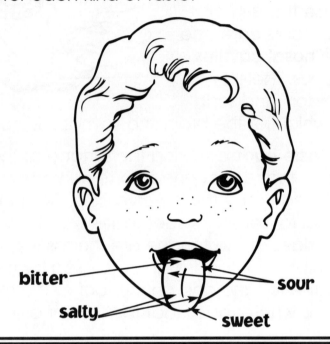

bitter   sour

salty   sweet

foods that taste sweet	foods that taste salty
_____	_____
_____	_____
_____	_____
foods that taste sour	foods that taste bitter
_____	_____
_____	_____
_____	_____

Name _____

Senses of Smell and Taste

Circle the words from the Word Bank in the puzzle. The words appear horizontally, vertically, diagonally, and backwards.

Word Bank

taste buds
bitter
nose
smell
sweet
nasal cavity
mucus
nostril
sour
taste
salty
tongue

```
t  n  s  w  e  e  t  n  s
l  a  v  b  m  u  n  o  w
e  s  s  i  r  u  o  s  e
m  a  s  t  m  o  s  d  b
s  l  v  t  e  u  t  u  i
m  c  e  t  c  s  r  b  t
e  a  r  u  r  m  i  e  t
l  v  m  v  g  e  l  t  e
l  i  u  g  s  n  l  s  r
e  t  u  o  n  g  o  a  l
e  y  n  t  s  a  l  t  y
```

Name _____

Going Undercover

The **skin** is the largest organ of the body. Skin is made up of two layers that provide a protective covering for the body. The top layer of skin is the **epidermis**. The epidermis has a thin, waterproof covering made of dead cells. Cells at the bottom of the epidermis divide and make new cells. These new cells push the old cells to the top of the epidermis. By the time the old cells reach the surface of the skin, they are dead. They serve as a protective coating for the skin. When you take a shower or change your clothes each day, millions of these dead cells get rubbed off. The body gets a new outer skin about every month.

Below the epidermis is the **dermis**, which is a much thicker layer of skin. The dermis contains hair, nerves, blood vessels, and glands. Oil glands keep skin from drying out. Sweat glands help to control the body's temperature. They produce sweat, or perspiration, which cools the body off when it gets too hot.

Answer each question.

1. What are the names of the two layers of skin?_____

   _____

2. How do dead cells get to the top of the epidermis?_____

   _____

   _____

3. What four things are found in the dermis?_____

   _____

4. What is the purpose of sweat glands?_____

   _____

Name _____

Skin Deep

Use the number code to label and color the diagram of the skin.

Number Code

1. Color the **dermis** yellow.
2. Color the **sweat glands** green.
3. Color the **hair** red.
4. Color the **epidermis** brown.
5. Color the **nerve endings** orange.
6. Color the **oil glands** blue.

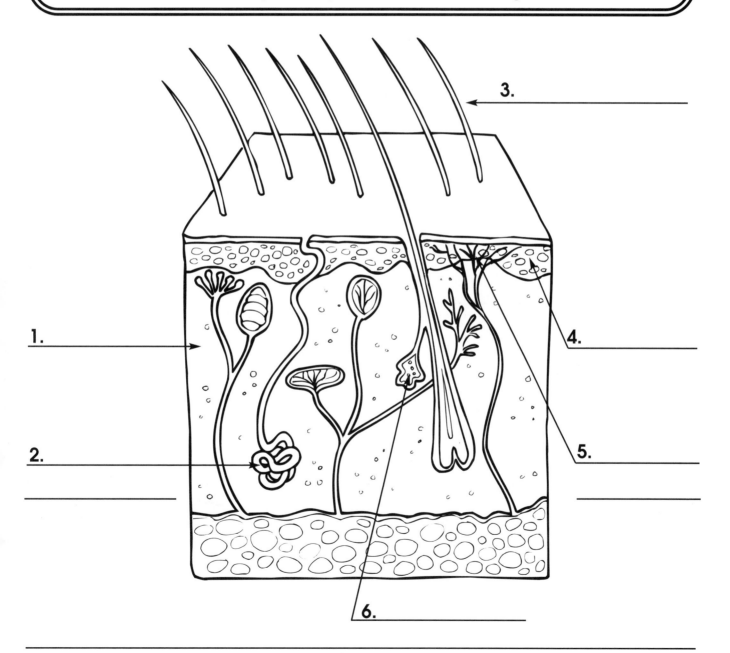

Name _____

Getting Under My Skin

Each of the following clues tells something about the skin. Use the words from the Word Bank to answer the questions.

Word Bank

oil gland	epidermis	sweat gland
hair	dermis	nerve

1. I start growing in the dermis. As I grow longer, I come out of the epidermis.

   What am I? _____

2. I help you feel what you touch. Without me you would not feel pain, pressure, heat, or cold.

   What am I? _____

3. I am a gland in the skin. What I produce helps to cool you down when you are too hot.

   What am I? _____

4. I am the top layer of the skin. Tough, dead cells help make me waterproof.

   What am I? _____

5. I am a thick layer of the skin. I contain hair, nerves, blood vessels, and glands.

   What am I? _____

6. I am another kind of gland. I keep the skin from drying out.

   What am I? _____

BEWARE POISON IVY!!

Name _____

Keep In Touch

Skin is the sensory organ for the sense of touch. There are many different types of **nerve endings** in the skin. Some of the nerve endings are used when touching something. There are also nerve endings that can detect heat, cold, pressure, and pain. Cells in the skin send messages along nerves to the **spinal cord**. The spinal cord then sends these messages to the touch center of the brain.

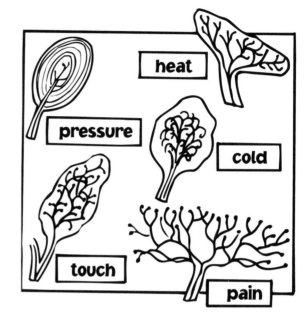

Answer each question.

1. What organ is used for the sense of touch?_____

2. What four sensations can the skin feel?_____

   _____

   _____

   _____

3. Where do cells send messages? _____

4. When you touch something, how does a message get to the brain to let you know what you are feeling?_____

   _____

   _____

   _____

Name _____

A Touching Experience

This diagram of skin shows the two layers of skin. It also illustrates the different types of nerves that allow feelings such as heat, cold, pain, or pressure.

Color the diagram. Then on the lines below, write at least two examples of feeling each sensation.

Color the **epidermis** brown.

Color the **dermis** yellow.

Color the nerve for **touch** green.

Color the nerve for **pain** orange.

Color the nerve for **pressure** pink.

Color the nerve for **heat** red.

Color the nerve for **cold** blue.

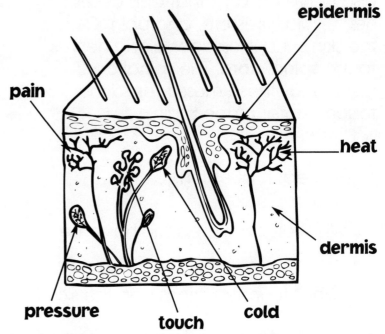

examples of feeling pain _____

_____

examples of feeling pressure _____

_____

examples of feeling heat _____

_____

examples of feeling cold _____

_____

Name _____

The Great Cover-Up

Circle the words from the Word Bank in the puzzle. The words appear horizontally, vertically, diagonally, and backwards.

Word Bank

cold	epidermis	nerves	pressure
skin	touch	dermis	heat
pain	sensation		

```
p  e  s  s  s  k  i  n  s
t  r  e  n  p  a  i  i  d
o  u  n  c  e  t  m  n  e
u  s  s  o  u  r  k  s  r
c  s  a  l  e  w  v  k  m
h  e  t  d  r  t  u  e  i
s  r  i  h  p  a  i  n  s
s  p  o  e  r  e  p  c  p
e  o  n  a  h  e  a  t  r
```

Name _____

Making Sense of the Senses

Write **T** for true or **F** for false in front of each statement about the senses. For each statement that is false, rewrite it on another piece of paper to make it a true statement.

_____ 1. There are only four senses.

_____ 2. The brain gets information about the world through the five senses.

_____ 3. Each of the sense organs is connected to the brain by nerves.

_____ 4. Teeth are the sense organs for the sense of taste.

_____ 5. The sense of smell helps when tasting food.

_____ 6. The tongue can only sense three tastes—sweet, bitter, and salty.

_____ 7. The skin is the sense organ for the sense of touch.

_____ 8. Skin can sense heat, cold, pressure, and pain.

_____ 9. All people have the same ability to see and hear.

Name _____

All About the Senses

Use the code to learn more interesting facts about the senses.

Code

A = 1	B = 2	C = 3	D = 4	E = 5	F = 6	G = 7
H = 8	I = 9	J = 10	K = 11	L = 12	M = 13	N = 14
O = 15	P = 16	Q = 17	R = 18	S = 19	T = 20	U = 21
V = 22	W = 23	X = 24	Y = 25	Z = 26		

1. This is the part of the eye that is sensitive to light. It is made up of about 106 million cells.

___ ___ ___ ___ ___ ___
18   5   20   9   14   1

2. A person can detect between 10,000 and 40,000 different types of these using about 20 million cells found inside the nose region.

___ ___ ___ ___ ___ ___
19   13   5   12   12   19

3. There are about 100,000 of these on the tongue and on the inside of your mouth and throat. They help you taste things.

___ ___ ___ ___ ___   ___ ___ ___ ___
20   1   19   20   5   2   21   4   19

4. The tube that connects the middle ear to the throat helps to keep air pressure the same on both sides of the eardrum. When flying in an airplane, changing air pressure makes air move quickly in the ears, causing the ears to do this.

___ ___ ___
16   15   16

5. Some areas of this organ are more sensitive to heat, cold, pressure, and pain. The body will shed about 40 pounds of this during its lifetime.

___ ___ ___ ___
19   11   9   14

Name _____

I Can Sense Something Wrong

For each of the sense organs there are four words listed. Three of the words tell about or belong to that sense organ; one does not. Circle the word that does not belong in each group.

1. eye (sense of sight)

   iris   cornea   pupil   cochlea

2. ear (sense of hearing)

   hammer   cochlea   retina   middle ear

3. skin (sense of touch)

   lens   dermis   epidermis   sweat gland

4. tongue (sense of taste)

   salty   sour   oil gland   taste buds

5. nose (sense of smell)

   nostrils   anvil   nasal cavity   mucus

Pssst!

Name _____

Healthy Habits

Write **T** for true or **F** for false in front of each statement about staying healthy. Rewrite each false sentence on another piece of paper to make it true.

_____ 1. Germs are harmful living things that can make someone sick.

_____ 2. Washing hands with soap and water before eating helps to keep germs out of food.

_____ 3. Washing hair using only water will keep it clean.

_____ 4. Glands near the eyes make tears to keep the eyes clean.

_____ 5. You should brush your teeth after every meal and before bedtime.

_____ 6. Plaque helps teeth stay healthy.

_____ 7. A hole in a tooth is called a cavity.

_____ 8. You should floss your teeth every day.

_____ 9. Regular exercise is important because it makes the heart and muscles strong.

_____ 10. All people require the same amount of sleep each night.

Name _____

nutrition

The body gets the **energy** it needs from **food**. High-energy foods like potatoes, bread, fruit, and cheese give the body a lot of energy. Low-energy foods like lettuce and tomatoes provide less energy.

There are six main kinds of **nutrients** in foods we eat: sugar and starch, fat, protein, vitamins, minerals, and water. **Sugar and starch** supply the body with quick energy. Apples, bananas, honey, and other sweet foods contain sugar. Bread, pasta, and potatoes, contain starch (carbohydrates). Any sugar and starch that the body does not use for energy is stored as fat.

Fat has more than twice as much energy as sugar or starch. The body stores fat to be used when it needs extra energy. Butter, milk, and cheese are some foods that have fat.

Protein is important for strong bones and muscles. The body cannot store protein, so it requires foods like meat, eggs, beans, or cheese every day to get the protein it needs.

Minerals help the body grow. **Calcium** is a mineral found in milk and cheese that helps to build strong bones and teeth. **Iron** is a mineral that is important for healthy blood. Liver and green vegetables are good sources of iron.

Vitamins help the body work properly. Most vitamins are named after letters of the alphabet. The body gets vitamin C from orange juice or other fruits. Vitamin D, which helps build strong bones and teeth, is found in milk.

The body cannot live without **water**. Over half of the body is made of water. People should drink six to eight glasses of water each day.

Answer each question.

1. How does the body get energy?_____

2. What are the names of the six main kinds of nutrients necessary for good health?_____

_____

3. What are two minerals that help the body grow?_____

4. Why is water so important for the body?_____

Name _____

Nutrition Knowledge

Write **T** for true or **F** for false in front of each statement about nutrition. Rewrite each false statement on another piece of paper to make it true.

_____ 1. The body gets the energy it needs from foods.

_____ 2. There are five main kinds of nutrients.

_____ 3. Sugar and starch supply the body with quick energy and can be found in apples, honey, and other sweet foods.

_____ 4. The body stores fat to be used when extra energy is needed.

_____ 5. Protein is important for strong bones and muscles, and it can be stored by the body.

_____ 6. Calcium and iron are two important minerals that help the body grow.

_____ 7. Most vitamins are named after letters of the alphabet.

_____ 8. People should drink six to eight glasses of water each day.

_____ 9. Over half of the body is made of water, and the body cannot live without it.

_____ 10. There are three main food groups.

Name _____

Name That Nutrient

Match each word or words in List I with its description from List II. Write the number in the box of the matching letter. To discover the magic number, add a row, column, or diagonal. The answer should always be the same!

List I

___ A. energy

___ B. protein

___ C. fat

___ D. minerals

___ E. vitamins

___ F. calcium

___ G. iron

___ H. water

___ I. carbohydrates

List II

1. found in meat, milk, and nuts; needed for strong bones and muscles; not stored by the body

2. high-energy foods; sugars and starches are some

3. help the body grow; calcium and iron are important ones

4. mineral that is important for healthy blood

5. help the body work properly; mostly named after letters of the alphabet

6. can be found in butter and oil; stored by the body

7. mineral that helps build strong bones and teeth

8. what food supplies for the body

9. 6 to 8 glasses of this is needed daily

A.	B.	C.
D.	E.	F.
G.	H.	I.

Magic Number _____

Name _____

Daily Requirements

The body will get the nutrients it needs to stay healthy if the guidelines of the food pyramid are followed. Study the pyramid below.

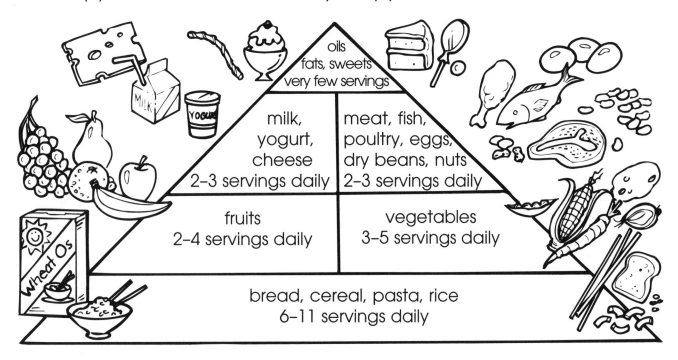

1. Write 1 beside each food that belongs in the bread, cereal, pasta, and rice group.

2. Write 2 beside each food that belongs in the fruit group.

3. Write 3 beside each food that belongs in the vegetable group.

4. Write 4 beside each food that belongs in the milk, yogurt, and cheese group.

5. Write 5 beside each food that belongs in the meat, fish, poultry, eggs, dry beans, and nuts group.

6. Write 6 beside each food that belongs in the oils, fats, and sweets group.

_____ chicken	_____ bagel	_____ eggs	_____ apple	_____ potato
_____ noodles	_____ orange	_____ steak	_____ butter	_____ salmon
_____ asparagus	_____ pecans	_____ tuna	_____ pudding	_____ tomato
_____ cauliflower	_____ cottage cheese		_____ cake	_____ beets

Name _____

Healthy Eating

Nutrients are the parts of food that the body needs for energy and growth. There are six main kinds of nutrients that help the body stay healthy. They are proteins, sugar and starch (carbohydrates), vitamins, minerals, water, and fats. Many foods contain more than one type of nutrient. Use the chart to keep track of everything you eat for one day. Then label each food item: 4 for very nutritious; 3 for nutritious; 2 for somewhat nutritious; 1 for not at all nutritious.

meals	nutrition level
breakfast	
lunch	
dinner	
snacks	

Name _____

You Are What You Eat

For each food group there are four foods listed. Three of the food items belong to that group; one does not. Circle the food that does not belong in each food group.

1. bread, cereal, pasta, and rice group

   waffle   spaghetti   orange   oatmeal

2. vegetable group

   broccoli   carrot   spinach   apple

3. fruit group

   turnip   banana   nectarine   peach

4. meat, fish, poultry, eggs, dry beans, and nuts group

   turkey   salmon   bagel   tuna

5. milk, yogurt, and cheese group

   cracker   yogurt   milk   cottage cheese

6. oils, fats, and sweets group

   hamburger   butter   margarine   candy

Name _____

Good Nutrition

Circle the words from the Word Bank in the puzzle. The words appear horizontally, vertically, diagonally, and backwards.

Word Bank

calcium	food	nutrients	sugar
carbohydrates	healthy	nutrition	vitamins
energy	iron	proteins	water
fats	minerals	starch	

```
w  s  i  h  c  r  a  t  s  r  c  v  v
a  c  p  r  o  t  e  i  n  s  f  i  e
c  a  r  b  o  h  y  d  r  a  t  e  s
s  l  w  u  b  n  i  e  t  a  i  m  t
n  c  e  r  a  g  u  s  n  e  v  i  n
i  i  e  n  u  t  r  i  t  i  o  n  e
i  u  k  n  f  w  n  w  t  j  s  e  i
t  m  o  o  e  s  a  a  a  i  t  r  r
o  e  o  d  r  r  w  t  g  r  a  a  t
r  d  d  f  t  u  g  e  e  o  f  l  u
p  h  e  a  l  t  h  y  s  r  y  s  n
```

Name _____

Idioms About the Human Body

An idiom is an expression with a meaning different from the literal meaning. Below are idioms or phrases that use names of body parts. Match the idiom with its meaning. Write the letter of the meaning next to the correct idiom.

Idiom

____ 1. Lend me a hand.

____ 2. Shake a leg.

____ 3. Put your foot down.

____ 4. Keep your fingers crossed.

____ 5. Eyes in back of your head

____ 6. Put your foot in your mouth.

____ 7. Head in the clouds

____ 8. Get your feet wet.

____ 9. Put your best foot forward.

____10. Jump down your throat

Meaning

a. daydreaming; lost in thought

b. ability to tell what is happening even if you are not looking

c. to help me out

d. trying to make a good impression

e. to hurry up; go faster

f. to be firm about something; not giving in

g. to wish for good luck or success

h. to say something you wish you had not

i. to do something for the first time

j. to talk or scream at someone in a sudden, angry way

Name _____

More Idioms About the Human Body

An idiom is an expression with a meaning different from the literal meaning. Below are idioms or phrases that use names of body parts. Match each idiom with its meaning. Write the letter of the meaning next to the correct idiom.

Idiom

_____ 1. No skin off my nose

_____ 2. Tongue-in-cheek

_____ 3. Head and shoulders above the rest

_____ 4. Green thumb

_____ 5. Get under their skin.

_____ 6. Break a leg.

_____ 7. Stick your neck out.

_____ 8. See eye to eye.

_____ 9. Rub elbows with someone.

_____ 10. Pull the wool over their eyes.

Meaning

a. far superior; much better

b. good luck; to do a great job

c. to agree or to have the same opinion

d. of no concern to you; it does not matter

e. to take a chance

f. intended as a joke; mocking; not serious

g. having a special talent for making plants grow well

h. to fool or trick people

i. to bother or upset someone

j. to be in the same place with someone or to associate with others

Name _____

Human Body Analogies

Analogies are comparisons. Fill in the blanks to complete each analogy about the human body.

1. Finger is to hand as toe is to _____ .

2. Hand is to arm as foot is to _____ .

3. Eye is to see as ear is to _____ .

4. Nose is to smell as tongue is to _____ .

5. Hand is to wrist as foot is to _____ .

6. Ribs are to lungs as skull is to _____ .

7. Knee is to leg as elbow is to _____ .

8. Teeth are to braces as eyes are to _____ .

9. Shoulder is to arm as hip is to _____ .

10. Inhale is to oxygen as exhale is to _____ .

Name _____

Bodily Sounds and Actions

Use the code to learn some interesting facts about the human body.

Code

A=1	B=2	C=3	D=4	E=5	F=6	G=7
H=8	I=9	J=10	K=11	L=12	M=13	N=14
O=15	P=16	Q=17	R=18	S=19	T=20	U=21
V=22	W=23	X=24	Y=25	Z=26		

1. This happens when the diaphragm suddenly flattens and causes air to pull into the lungs through the voice box, making a funny noise.

   __ __ __ __ __ __
   8 9 3 3 21 16

2. If the body suddenly gets cold, it makes the muscles of the skin contract causing your hair to "stand on end," which causes these.

   __ __ __ __ __   __ __ __ __ __
   7 15 15 19 5   2 21 13 16 19

3. When the nerve endings in the nose become irritated, the body will do this as the muscles in the eyelids, throat, vocal cords, and chest contract.

   __ __ __ __ __ __
   19 14 5 5 26 5

4. If food goes to the windpipe while eating, the body will do this. It is an automatic muscle contraction that sends a sudden, strong rush of air from the lungs.

   __ __ __ __ __
   3 15 21 7 8

5. Sometimes, especially after eating a meal, air from the stomach suddenly comes up through the esophagus and goes out through the mouth, making this noise.

   __ __ __ __ __ or __ __ __ __
   2 5 12 3 8   2 21 18 16

Name _____

Writing Activity

A Cinquain Poem

A cinquain is a non-rhyming poem that has five lines. Write a cinquain poem about a major organ of the body by following the instructions. After your poem is finished, use a piece of colored construction paper and cut it into the shape of the organ you have written about. Cut out your poem and paste it onto the construction paper background.

Line 1: one word; the name of an organ

Line 2: two words; a description of Line 1

Line 3: three words; an action that the organ performs

Line 4: four words; feelings about Line 1

Line 5: one word; a synonym or a word referring back to Line 1

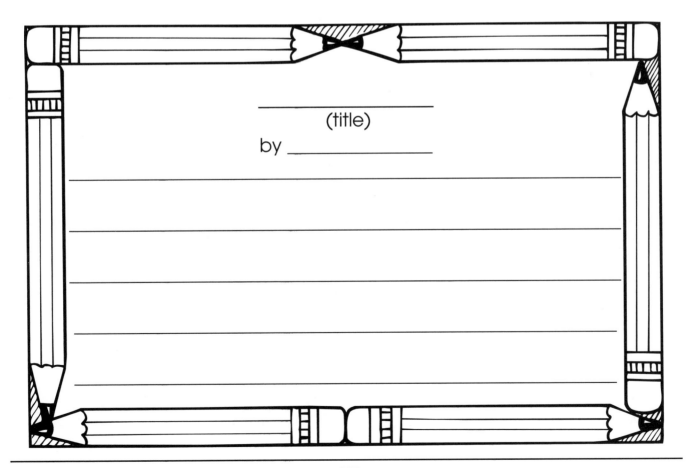

_____
(title)
by _____

Name _____

A Body Makeover

Now that you have studied the systems of the body and the organs that they contain, create a model of your body and the organs inside.

Materials needed:

- pasta shells
- dry beans
- pipe cleaners
- cotton balls
- balloons
- spaghetti
- plastic packing peanuts
- pretzels
- tissue paper
- miniature marshmallows
- raisins
- licorice

Instructions:

1. Have a partner trace a complete outline of your body on large butcher or newsprint paper using a pencil. Trace the pencil markings with a black marker.

2. Cut out the outline of your body.

3. Cut out the body patterns on pages 117-123. On the back of each, write the following:
   - A. the name of the system of the body to which that body part belongs
   - B. the job or function of that body part

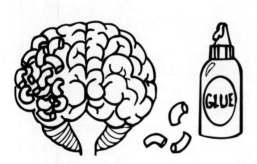

4. Use materials from the list above to glue on top of each body part to give it color, texture, or a 3-D effect.

5. Cut out the names of the different body parts and glue each name on the body part after you have designed it.

6. Place the body parts in the proper positions on the outline of your body. Glue the tabs down to keep the body parts in place.

7. Quiz yourself or your partner by identifying the system of the body to which each organ or body part belongs, and its function in the body.

Body Patterns

Note: Each body part needs to include a tab so that only the tab is glued to the body outline.

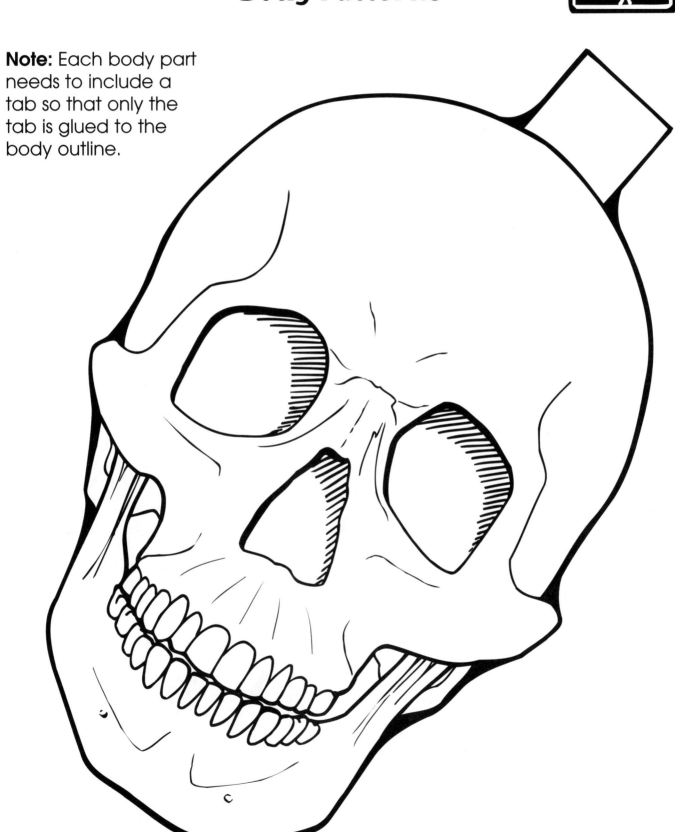

Body Patterns

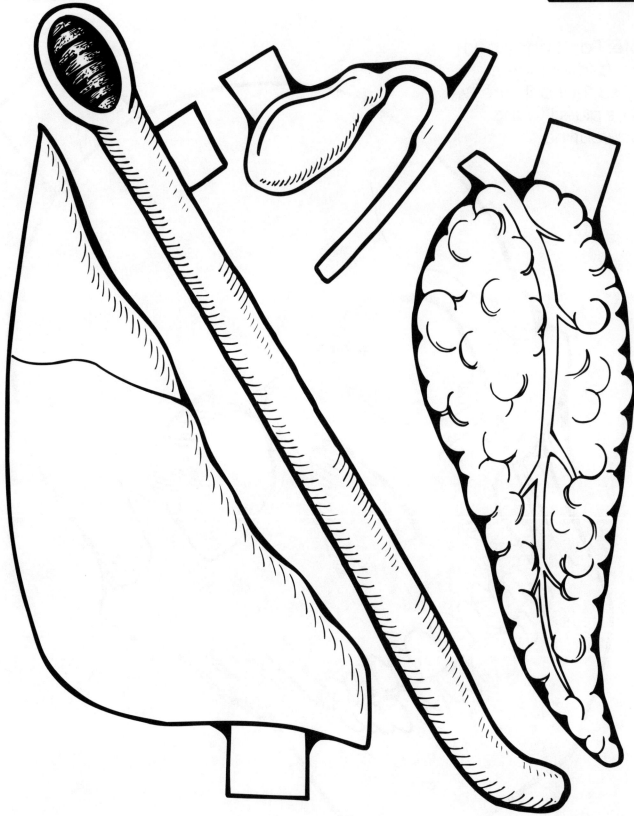

Body Patterns

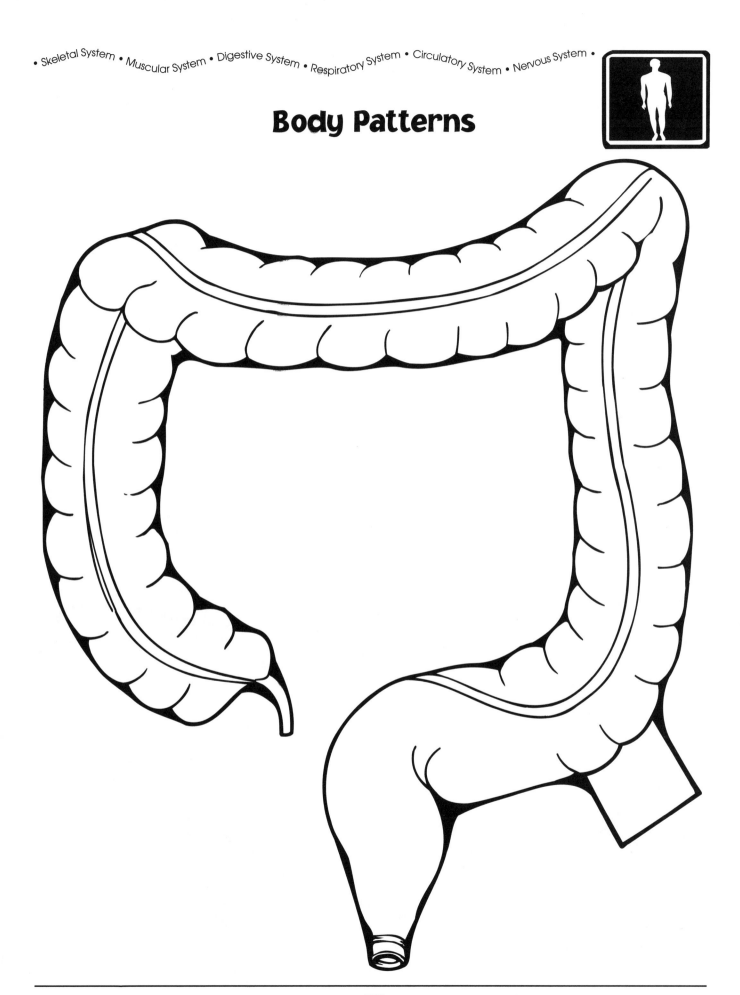

Body Patterns

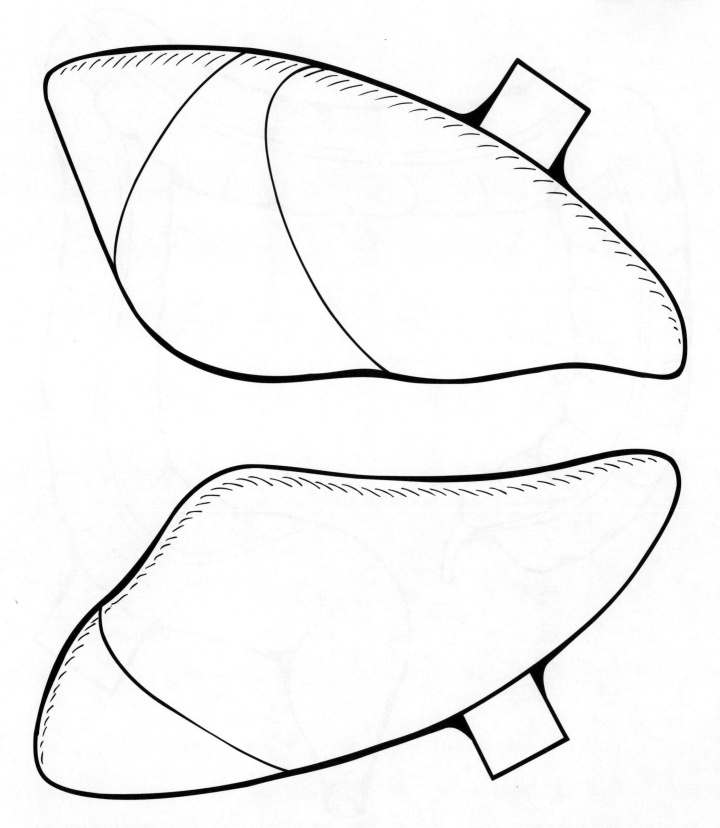

Body Patterns

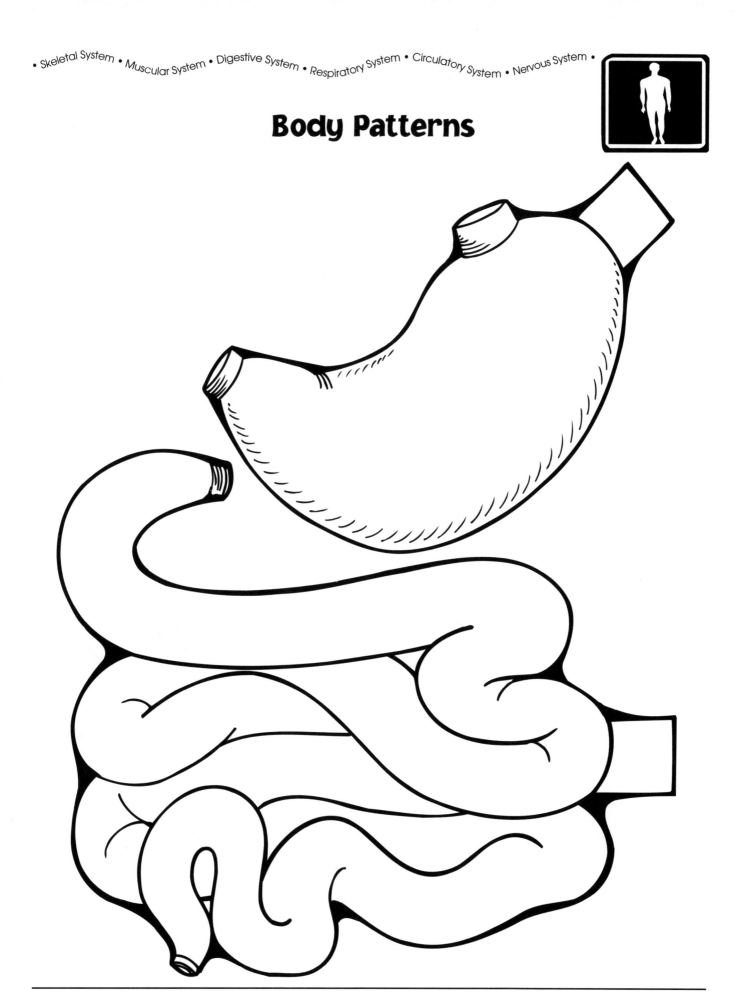

121

Body Patterns

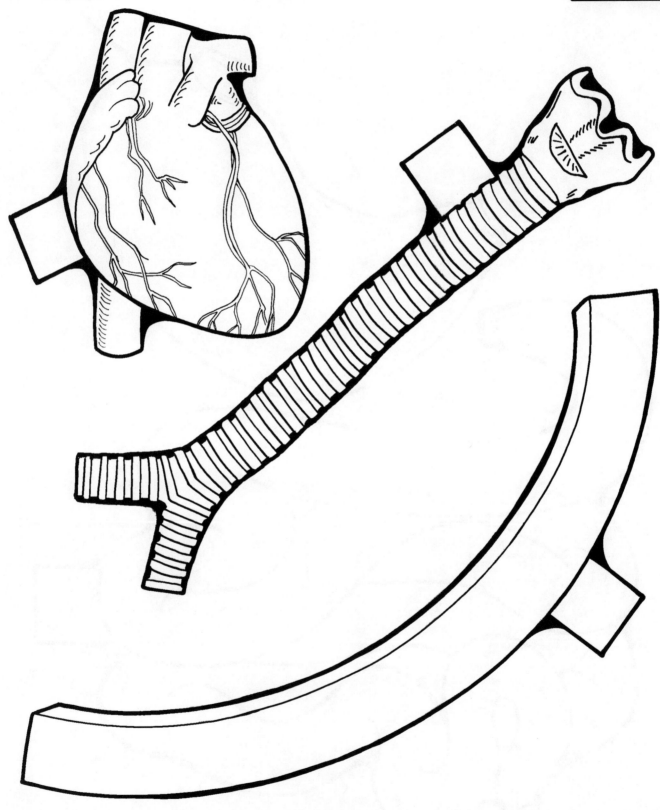

Body Patterns

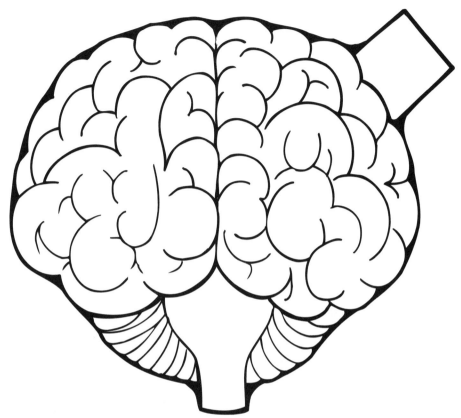

skull	brain	heart
liver	stomach	trachea
esophagus	pancreas	diaphragm
lungs	gallbladder	
small intestine	large intestine	

Answer Key

Page 4

1. bone cell; 2. muscle cell;
3. epithelial cell; 4. white blood cell;
5. red blood cell; 6. nerve cell

Page 9

1. Skeletal System: bones, joints;
2. Muscular System: muscles, tendons;
3. Digestive System: stomach, small intestine, large intestine; 4. Respiratory System: trachea, lungs, diaphragm;
5. Circulatory System: veins, arteries, heart; 6. Nervous System: brain, spinal cord, nerves

Page 10

1. heart; 2. ribs; 3. gallbladder; 4. large intestine; 5. liver; 6. pancreas

Page 15

Charts will vary.

Page 16

1. The functions of the skeletal system are support, movement, and protection.; 2. Cartilage is a rubbery tissue found where two bones meet.; 3. Ligaments connect the bones in the joints and keep them in place.; 4. Bone marrow is a soft tissue that makes new blood cells.

Page 17

1. collarbone; 2. breast bone; 3. ribs; 4. hipbone; 5. thighbone; 6. foot bones; 7. skull; 8. jawbone; 9. neck bones; 10. upper arm bone; 11. backbone; 12. lower arm bone; 13. hand bones; 14. kneecap; 15. shinbone; 16. calf bone

Page 18

1. c; 2. d; 3. b; 4. a

Page 19

1. fixed joints; 2. ball-and-socket joints; 3. hinge joints; 4. pivot joints; 5. gliding joint

Page 20

1. T ; 2. F, The skeletal system helps the body move.; 3. T ; 4. T; 5. T; 6. F, Cartilage is a rubbery tissue and is not the same as bone.; 7. T; 8. T; 9. F, Bones are made of calcium and phosphorous.; 10. T

Page 21

1. bones; 2. steel; 3. thigh; 4. hands and feet; 5. ear; 6. funny bone

Page 22

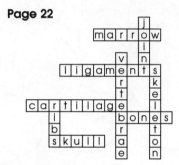

Page 23

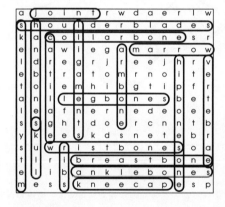

Page 24

Charts will vary.

Page 25

1. The muscular system controls movement in the body.; 2. A voluntary muscle can be controlled by thinking about it, while an involuntary muscle cannot be consciously controlled.; 3. Skeletal muscles are attached to bones by tendons. They move the bones by working in opposite pairs.; 4. The types of muscle are skeletal, smooth, and cardiac.

Page 26

1. shoulder muscles; 2. triceps;
3. head muscles; 4. chest muscles;
5. biceps; 6. stomach muscles;
7. thigh muscles; 8. calf muscles

Page 27

1. c; 2. a; 3. b; 4. cardiac muscle;
5. smooth muscle; 6. skeletal muscle

Page 28

1. T; 2. T; 3. F, You can control voluntary muscle like those in your arm or leg.; 4. T; 5. F, Tendons are tough bands of tissue attached to bones.; 6. T; 7. T; 8. T

Page 29

1. face; 2. Achilles tendon; 3. muscles; 4. oxygen; 5. shivers; 6. biceps

Page 30

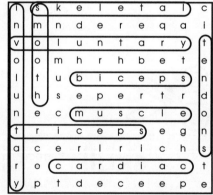

Page 31

1. move; 2. muscle; 3. cardiac;
4. voluntary; 5. skeletal; 6. smooth;
7. tendons; 8. involuntary

Page 32

1. bicep; 2. tricep; 3. when one muscle contracts, the other relaxes.

Page 33

Charts will vary.

Answer Key

Page 34

1. The digestive system changes food into a form that can be used by the cells of the body.; 2. Teeth break the food into smaller pieces, and saliva makes the food soft and wet.; 3. The organs of the digestive system are esophagus, stomach, small intestine, large intestine, liver, gallbladder, and pancreas.

Page 35

1. upper canine; 2. upper molars; 3. lower premolars; 4. upper incisors; 5. upper premolars; 6. lower canines; 7. lower molars; 8. lower incisors

Page 36

1. crown; 2. pulp chamber; 3. root; 4. enamel; 5. dentin; 6. nerves and blood vessels

Page 37

1. crown; 2. root; 3. pulp chamber; 4. dentin, 5. cavity; enamel

Page 38

1. b; 2. c; 3. d; 4. f; 5. h; 6. g; 7. e; 8. a

Page 39

1. esophagus; 2. liver; 3. gallbladder; 4. large intestine; 5. teeth; 6. tongue; 7. stomach; 8. pancreas; 9. small intestine

Page 40

1. F, Digestion begins in the mouth.; 2. T; 3. F, Your teeth and tongue are part of the digestive system.; 4. F, There are muscles in your stomach.; 5. T; 6. T; 7. T; 8. F, The small intestine is the longest part of the digestive system.

Pages 41

A. 6; B. 7; C. 2; D. 1; E. 5; F. 9; G. 8; H. 3; I. 4; Magic number: 15

Page 42

1. elephants; 2. stomach growls; 3. teeth; 4. small intestine; 5. saliva; 6. stomach

Page 43

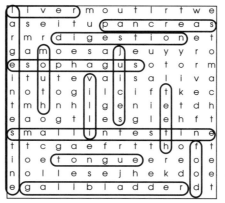

Page 44

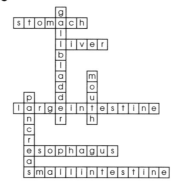

Page 45

Correct order: 7; 1; 10; 3; 2; 4; 8; 5; 9; 6

Page 46

1. The color changes indicate the presence of starch.; 2. Answers will vary.; 3. The body needs starch for energy.

Page 47

Charts will vary.

Page 48

1. The respiratory system brings in oxygen and removes carbon dioxide.; 2. The main organs of this system are the trachea and lungs.; 3. The diaphragm controls inhalation and exhalation by expanding and contracting.; 4. Oxygen is needed by the body because it is used by the cells to burn food for energy.

Page 49

1. throat; 2. bronchial tubes; 3. lungs; 4. nose and mouth; 5. voice box; 6. windpipe; 7. diaphragm

Page 50

1. f; 2. d; 3. a; 4. b; 5. e; 6. c

Page 51

1. T; 2. F, The body needs oxygen to survive and gives off carbon dioxide as a waste product.; 3. T; 4. T; 5. T; 6. F, People have two lungs.; 7. T; 8. T; 9. F, A person inhales when breathing in.; 10. T

Page 52

1. nose hairs; 2. mucus; 3. alveoli; 4. breathes; 5. water vapor; 6. smoking

Page 53

A. 5; B. 10; C. 3; D. 4; E. 6; F. 8; G. 9; H. 2; I. 7; Magic number: 18

Page 54

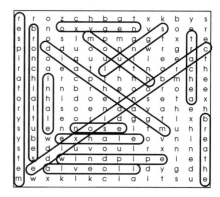

Page 55

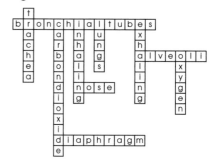

Answer Key

Page 56
Results and conclusions will vary.

Page 57
1. The top balloon is like the lungs, and the bottom balloon is like the diaphragm.; 2. The lungs expand and you inhale when the diaphragm flattens out. When the diaphragm returns to its dome shape, air is exhaled from the lungs.

Page 58
Charts will vary.

Page 59
1. The circulatory system carries materials throughout the body.; 2. The main types of blood vessels are arteries, veins, and capillaries.; 3. The main parts of the circulatory system are the heart, blood vessels, and blood.; 4. Solid particles that make up blood are red blood cells, white blood cells, and platelets.

Page 60
1. b; 2. a; 3. d; 4. f; 5. e; 6. g; 7. c; 8. right atrium; 9. right ventricle; 10. left atrium; 11. left ventricle

Page 62
1. T; 2. T; 3. F, The heart is a muscle.; 4. T; 5. T; 6. F, Arteries, veins, and capillaries are different sizes.; 7. T; 8. F, White blood cells help the body attack germs and fight disease.; 9. F, Red blood cells carry the oxygen in the body.; 10. T

Page 63
1. heartbeat; 2. pins and needles; 3. pear; 4. blood vessels; 5. white blood cells; 6. heart

Page 64
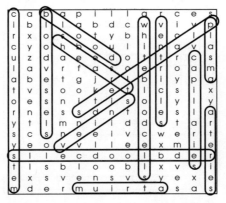

Page 65
Correct order: 5; 1; 4; 6; 2; 7; 3

Page 66
Results and conclusions will vary.

Page 67
Charts will vary.

Page 68
1. The nervous system receives and carries messages throughout the body.; 2. The brain and spinal cord are the main organs of the nervous system.; 3. The main parts of the brain are the cerebrum, cerebellum, and medulla. The cerebrum controls learning, memory, and reasoning. The cerebellum controls balance and coordination. The medulla controls involuntary body actions.

Page 69
1. brain; 2. spinal cord; 3. nerves

Page 70
1. cerebrum; 2. cerebellum; 3. spinal cord; 4. medulla

Page 71
1. T; 2. T; 3. T; 4. F, The cerebrum is the largest part of the brain.; 5. F, The cerebellum controls balance and coordination.; 6. T; 7. F, The peripheral nervous system and central nervous system are not the same thing.; 8. T

Page 72
1. spinal cord; 2. cells; 3. nerves; 4. signals; 5. brain

Page 73
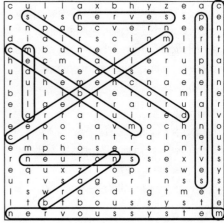

Page 74
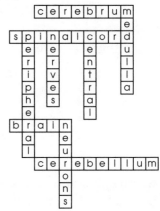

Page 75
Answers will vary.

Page 76
Results and conclusions will vary.

Page 77
Charts will vary.

Answer Key

Page 78

1. The cornea is the front part of the eye.; 2. The pupil is the opening through which light enters the eye.; 3. The iris is the colored part of the eye that controls how much light comes through the pupil.; 4. The lens is the clear part of the eye that bends light and reflects it into the retina.; 5. The retina is the back wall of the eye where light hits cells and nerve endings pick up messages. The messages are sent to the brain where they are interpreted.

Page 79

1. cornea; 2. pupil; 3. iris; 4. lens; 5. retina; 6. nerve

Page 80

1. eye; 2. cornea; 3. iris; 4. pupil; 5. lens; 6. retina; 7. optic nerve

Page 81

Page 82

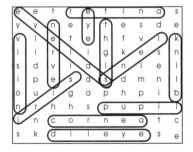

Page 83

Results and conclusions will vary.

Page 84

Results and conclusions will vary.

Page 85

1. The three parts of the ear are the outer ear, the middle ear, and the inner ear.; 2. The eardrum is a thin sheet of tissue located at the end of the ear canal.; 3. The three small bones in the inner ear are the hammer, anvil, and stirrup.; 4. In the inner ear, vibrations cause the liquid and the nerve endings to move. The nerve endings signal the brain, and a sound is heard.

Page 86

1. outer ear; 2. ear canal; 3. eardrum; 4. middle ear; 5. inner ear

Page 87

1. ear; 2. outer ear; 3. ear canal; 4. eardrum; 5. middle ear; 6. cochlea

Page 88

1. outer ear; 2. eardrum; 3. stirrup; 4. ear canal; 5. cochlea; 6. ear; drums; noise

Page 89

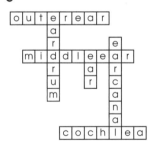

Page 90

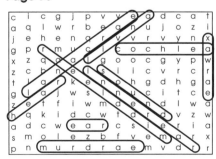

Page 91

1. The nose takes in air that carries odors, and the odors travel to the nasal cavities.; 2. Taste buds are cells that are connected to nerve endings. The tongue has 10,000 taste buds.; 3. Taste buds can detect sweetness on the tip of the tongue, salty on the middle and sides of the tongue, sour on the back sides of the tongue and on the roof of the mouth, and bitter on the very back of the tongue.

Page 92

Answers will vary.

Page 93

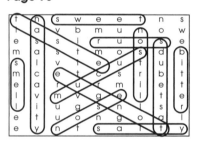

Page 94

1. The two layers of the skin are the dermis and epidermis.; 2. New cells are made at the bottom of the epidermis so the old cells are pushed up.; 3. Hair, nerves, blood vessels, and glands are found in the dermis.; 4. Sweat glands produce sweat to help the body cool off when it gets too hot.

Page 95

1. dermis; 2. sweat glands; 3. hair; 4. epidermis; 5. nerve endings; 6. oil glands

Page 96

1. hair; 2. nerve; 3. sweat gland; 4. epidermis; 5. dermis; 6. oil gland

Answer Key

Page 97

1. Skin is used for the sense of touch.; 2. Skin can feel heat, pressure, cold, and pain.; 3. Cells in the skin send messages to the spinal cord.; 4. The spinal cord sends the messages to the touch center of the brain.

Page 98

Answers will vary.

Page 99

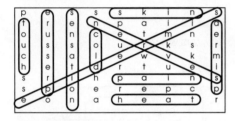

Page 100

1. F, There are five senses.; 2. T; 3. T; 4. F, The tongue is the sense organ for the sense of taste.; 5. T; 6. F, The tongue can sense four tastes– sweet, salty, sour, and bitter.; 7. T; 8. T; 9. F, People have different abilities to see and hear.

Page 101

1. retina; 2. smells; 3. taste buds; 4. pop; 5. skin

Page 102

1. cochlea; 2. retina; 3. lens; 4. oil gland; 5. anvil

Page 103

1. T; 2. T; 3. F, Washing hair with soap and water will keep it clean.; 4. T; 5. T; 6. F, Plaque makes teeth unhealthy.; 7. T; 8. T; 9. T; 10. F, People require different amounts of sleep each night.

Page 104

1. The body gets energy from food.; 2. The six main nutrients are sugar and starch, fat, protein, minerals, vitamins, and water.; 3. Calcium and iron are two minerals that help the body grow.; 4. Water is important because over half of the body is made of water.

Page 105

1. T; 2. F, There are six main kinds of nutrients.; 3. T; 4. T; 5. F, Protein is important for strong bones and muscles, and it cannot be stored by the body.; 6. T; 7. T; 8. T; 9. T; 10. F, There are four main food groups.

Page 106

A. 8; B. 1; C. 6; D. 3; E. 5; F. 7; G. 4; H. 9; I. 2; Magic number: 15

Page 107

1. noodles, bagel; 2. orange, apple, tomato; 3. asparagus, cauliflower, potato, beets; 4. cottage cheese; 5. chicken, pecans, eggs, steak, tuna, salmon; 6. butter, pudding, cake

Page 108

Charts will vary.

Page 109

1. orange; 2. apple; 3. turnip; 4. bagel; 5. cracker; 6. hamburger

Page 110

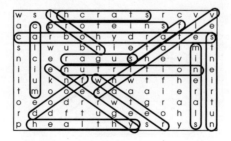

Page 111

1. c; 2. e; 3. f; 4. g; 5. b; 6. h; 7. a; 8. i; 9. d; 10. j

Page 112

1. d; 2. f; 3. a; 4. g; 5. i; 6. b; 7. e; 8. c; 9. j; 10. h

Page 113

1. foot; 2. leg; 3. hear; 4. taste; 5. ankle; 6. brain; 7. arm; 8. glasses; 9. leg; 10. carbon dioxide

Page 114

1. hiccup; 2. goose bumps; 3. sneeze; 4. cough; 5. belch or burp

Page 115

Poems will vary.